C000221367

On a Bat's Wing

On a Bat's Wing
Poems about Bats

Edited by
Michael Baron

Five Leaves Publications
www.fiveleaves.co.uk

On a Bat's Wing
Poems about Bats
Edited by Michael Baron

Published in 2007 by Five Leaves Publications,
PO Box 8786, Nottingham NG1 9AW
info@fiveleaves.co.uk
www.fiveleaves.co.uk

ISBN: 978 1905512270

Five Leaves gratefully acknowledges financial support
from Arts Council England

Illustrations: cover "Bat outa Hell"
by Roseanne Jones/Artamatik www.artamatik.co.nz,
bat illustrations Emily Faccini save for Carri Swann on p. 58.

Designed and typeset by Four Sheets Design and Print
Printed in Great Britain

Five Leaves is a member of Inpress, representing independent
publishers (www.inpressbooks.co.uk)

Contents

Preface by John Altringham   8

Introduction by Michael Baron   11

William Shakespeare   *from* The Tempest   15
Catriona O'Reilly   A Lecture upon the Bat   16
Les Murray   Bats' Ultrasound   18
Matthew Sweeney   The Bats   19
Menna Elfyn   The Year of the Bat, 1986
                         (translated from the Welsh by
                         Gillian Clarke)   21
Victoria Field   My Affair with the Bat   23
Stevie Krayer   Iaith Fyw (Living Language)   24
Graham Mort   Batsville   25
Chris Preddle   Bat   26
Michael Longley   The Bat   27
Ted Hughes   9 Willow Street   28
Gillian Clarke   Pipistrelle   32
Geoffrey Hill   Vocations   33
La Fontaine, derived
from Aesop's Fables:
(translated by Edward   The Bat and the Two Weasels
Marsh)   34
Christopher Pilling   Say What You Are   36
Geoffrey Grigson   Sixteen Dogs, Cats, Rats and Bats   38
George MacBeth   Bats   39
Frank Jacobs   The Bat   40
Roy Fisher   Rat-bat *from* Figures from
                         Anansi Company   41
Angela Leighton   Sonar   42
Martin Langford   Silky Oak   43
Tinker Mather   The Bats   44
Penelope Shuttle   The Bat of Totality   45
Jacob Polley   Bats   46
Ted Hughes   Karlsbad Caverns   47
Sue Hubbard   Bat   49
Michael Laskey   The Present   50
Robert Nye   A Bat in a Box   51
Susan Wicks   Protected Species   52

Ted Hughes	The Bat	53
Kathleen Jamie	Pipistrelles	54
John Clare	*from* Childhood	55
Mike Johnson	Darkness	56
Ogden Nash	The Bat	57
John Lucas	Are Umbrellas Really Bats?	58
Roger McGough	Uncle Bram	59
John Tranter	Bats	60
John Ashbery	Local Legend	61
John Berryman	Dream Song '63	62
Matthew Francis	Off the Ground	63
Richard Wilbur	Mind	64
Roy Fuller	Enigmas Part III	65
Jo Shapcott	Life	66
Geraldine Green	Bats	68
Walter de la Mare	All but blind	69
Edward Lear	B was a Bat	70
Stevie Krayer	The Power of Words	71
Theodore Roethke	The Bat	72
Emily Dickinson	The Bat	73
Ruth Pitter	The Bat	74
D.H. Lawrence	Man and Bat	75
D.J. Enright	In Memoriam R.G.C.	81
John Updike	Zoo Bats	82
Jeredith Merrin	Bat Ode (Downtown Columbus, Rush Hour)	85
Randall Jarrell	A Bat is Born	86
Elizabeth Barrett	The Absence of Bats	87
Seamus Heaney	A Bat in the Road	89
Pat Borthwick	Learning About Bats	90
Vicki Feaver	Bats	92
Edith Sitwell	The Bat	94
George MacBeth	Lady Dracula	95
Elizabeth Jennings	The Bats' Plea	97
John Kinsella	They Say of Bats...	98
Carole Baldock	Assault & Battery	99
Caroline Carver	ratbat	100
Gill Nicholson	Daubenton's Bats	101
Tamar Yoseloff	Bat Samba	102
William Allingham	*from* Little Verses for Very Little Children	103

Dorothy Cowlin	A Bat	104
Stevie Smith	The Fairy Bell	105
Ovid	*from* The Feast of Bacchus	
(translated by	(Metamorphoses)	
Arthur Golding)		106
John Altringham	Echolocation	108
Michael Baron	Vol de Nuit	109
Grevel Lindop	Echoes	110
Christopher Pilling	I'll Go So far	112
Jane Kenyon	The Bat	114
Les Murray	Fruit Bat Colony by Day	115

Biographies/Contributors Notes 116

Preface

Because most are small and nocturnal, bats have largely
escaped our notice, other than as a spark for myth and
superstition. Yet they are one of evolution's big success
stories. Bats have been around long enough to witness the
demise of the dinosaurs. We have little idea precisely how
they evolved or what early bats looked like, since few of
their delicate skeletons have survived as fossils. But, with
the evolution of a rich variety of flowering plants, the bats,
from their obscure beginnings, blossomed too, thriving on
the plants themselves and on the abundant diversity of
insects associated with them.

There are now over 1,100 species of bat on the Earth.
They inhabit every continent except Antarctica, every
temperate and tropical island but the most remote and
every major habitat but the open seas and frozen wastes.
Most of them feed on insects, many others on fruit and
nectar, but there are bats that feed on fish, amphibians,
reptiles, birds, and other mammals, including other bats.

The small nectar-feeding bats hover in front of flowers
like nocturnal hummingbirds and like hummingbirds will
eat insects too. Most insect-eaters feed in flight on the
small and largely defenceless, but some will tackle larger
and more formidable invertebrates on the ground, such as
scorpions and giant, predatory centipedes. Just three
species feed on blood, leaving all bats unjustifiably tar-
nished. There are cave-roosting species that form colonies
ten million strong and solitary, tree-roosting species. Bats
are small mammals with big ideas: long-lived and typically
producing only one baby a year, they lead the complex,
caring lives typical of much bigger mammals, with intri-
cate social systems and behaviours.

After the pterosaurs and the birds, they are the only ver-
tebrates to have evolved powered flight, which has given
them mastery of the night sky. As nocturnal hunters, bats
can have an acute and multi-faceted perception of the

world. Some have eyes capable of seeing by starlight and moonlight. Many can hear an insect walking across a leaf. Most use echolocation, a form of sonar that can detect a flying insect at twenty metres, calculate its speed and direction of flight in a fraction of a second, and even tell the bat what type of insect it is. Echolocation, in combination with an acute sense of smell, leads bats to night-opening flowers and ripe fruit. Like bees, some bats are attracted to flowers that glow in ultra-violet. Infra-red detectors around the nose guide vampire bats to their next meal. Bats sense the world in ways we can barely imagine.

As bats evolved and diversified they reached out from the hospitable tropics to exploit the rich, temperate summers, but they had to find ways to avoid the harsh winters. So these undoubtedly very hot-blooded mammals learned to turn down the thermostat. A hibernating bat can spend half the year in deep sleep, chilled almost to freezing point. Heart rate, breathing rate and metabolic rate are at a near standstill, conserving energy until the insects return in the spring.

Knowing little or none of this, humans had ephemeral encounters with bats for thousands of years, inspiring wonder, awe, contempt and fear. At the same time pragmatic, humans nevertheless utilised bats for food, medicine and magic. Around the world a complex mythology surrounds bats. In Central America, the real home of vampire bats, the Mayans worshipped Zotz, the vampire bat god, guardian of the underworld through which humans must pass after death. In ancient Greece, bats were associated with Persephone, wife of Hades. A bat is the guardian of death in some Australian Aboriginal cultures and it was by frightening this bat from its perch by a cave that humans unleashed death upon themselves. In China, bats represent the five great happinesses: health, wealth, good luck, long life and tranquility, depicted symbolically in the Wu-Fu, five bats around a peach tree, an emblem still common on Chinese pottery. Bats are also modern icons: Batman, the Bacardi logo and the Lamborghini

Murciélago. Bats are not rare in literature either, from the Bible and Aristotle to Bram Stoker and Lewis Carroll. However, they play minor parts that only occasionally reflect their true nature. Even in works of reference they were frequently misunderstood. Oliver Goldsmith in his *History of the Earth and Animated Nature* (1774) accused them of sneaking into the larder to steal the fatty bacon. However, he felt that their "unsteady wobbling motion, amuse the imagination, and add one figure more to the pleasing group of animated nature". I'm glad to say that this, together with their industrious pursuit of insects exonerated them. Randall Jarrell's *The Bat Poet*, does, for me, capture much of the real essence of a bat, as do the drawings of Maurice Sendak that illustrate the story. It is therefore fitting that the bat in the story seeks to tell others, through his poems, how he sees his world and in the process, reveals something of himself.

Professor John Altringham
Institute of Integrative and Comparative Biology
University of Leeds

Men, Women, Bats — Poetry

Why an anthology of poems about bats by poets great and small, famous and obscure? The answer has to be that wherever bats hang about, so do poets. This anthology celebrates the bat in words. Bat poems have swarmed towards me from the length and breadth of the country, and from America, Australia and New Zealand. Some great poets and great poems have had to be excluded because they only touch briefly on bats but those poems that are in the anthology make an extraordinary tribute.

Bats are with us in town and country, in suburban roof, ancient mansion, tumbled barn, woodland, cave, desert and rain forest. They are the visible, silent neighbours of summer evenings, mysterious in life cycle, amazing in physiological mastery of the night. One poet, Michael Longley, describes bats as "wonderful, beautiful, humbling". And so they are, though historically they haven't always been seen as such. In 1981, when the Wildlife and Protection of the Countryside Act protected bats from various human interventions, Auberon Waugh could only say, "I do not suppose there are more than a couple of hundred people [who] could give a hoot if every bat in the kingdom dropped down dead. I, for one, would rejoice.... Like horseflies, they have absolutely nothing to recommend them. They are dirty, smelly and frightening." Among the poems represented here, only D.H. Lawrence seems to belong to Waugh's bat-hating fraternity. Meanwhile, the Bat Conservation Trust, who will receive all royalties from this anthology, and the Bat Conservation International (USA) now boast more than fifteen thousand members between them worldwide.

In Western Judaeo-Christian tradition, bats are deemed a bad thing. The bad press started in Babylon, encouraged by early labelling as unclean in "Leviticus" and

11

"Deuteronomy". And in "Isaiah", as an integral part of an agenda of humbling by the Lord, the prophet has the people throwing "away to the moles and to the bats their idols of silver...". Later in the Biblical epoch, the apocryphal "Book of Baruch" has the priests in Babylon, faces blackened by smoke, with "bats, swallows and birds" on their heads, while their hearts are gnawed away by "things creeping out of the earth". Islam is more tolerant; according to Muslim belief, bats were created by Christ and flew gratefully around him at sundown to ensure he knew what time it was!

The poet Ovid described in his "Metamorphoses" how the daughters of Minyas of Orchomenos were turned into bats for breaking Bacchus' high feast contemptuously. Homer used a bat as a metaphor for strength (Ulysses, tossed about between Scylla and Charybdis, hangs on to a fig tree trunk like a bat). Aesop's tale of the bat and the two weasels as re-interpreted by La Fontaine features a clever bat escaping trouble, but in general, classical literature is dotted with bats who were associates of darkness, companions to devils and imps.

Not until Shakespeare is there a poet who writes a song for a bat, with Ariel, a free-loading traveller, leaving his cowslip to mount the bat's back for time off from Prospero's employment. Looking ahead to the Victorians, Tennyson's "black bat night" (in "Maud") is a throwback to ancient associations.

Meanwhile, in the USA, Emily Dickinson's bat anticipates a gentler approach. Hers is a "small umbrella quaintly halved", an "elate philosopher".

In the UK and Ireland, from where the majority of the poems are drawn, the bats under scrutiny are small-winged mammals. In the USA and the Antipodes, it is the larger species that poets often celebrate. As Professor John Altringham writes in his Preface, there are more than 1,100 species worldwide. More poems and songs remain to be gathered in and translated.

The poets in this anthology cast bats in many roles — it

12

is the meeting between poet and bat, the meaning of the bat in the human context, that seems uppermost. Where Lawrence is a sensitive observer of bat behaviour (he notices a "strange parabola" before the bat's departure), for Randall Jarrell bats are fun. As they are for Ogden Nash and Theodore Roethke — "mice with wings can wear a human face". Ruth Pitter rescues hers from a cat. Ted Hughes tries to save a bat on Boston Common which, in turn, provides him with a symbol of, or key to, his own suffering. There are other narrow escapes for bats, but some are not so lucky.

"What is it like to be a bat?" some of the poets ask. Jo Shapcott explores "my life as a bat" and Les Murray goes as far as he dares into identity change, trying out how it sounds, feels. There are sensual, erotic bats — as in Sue Hubbard's "heart between hot sheets" and innumerable bats that set up an echo between their world and that of the poet.

Further comment on the diversity in the anthology will spoil the pleasure of engagement and discovery for the reader. He or she may hereafter look at the bat with greater curiosity and — I hope — respect for its venerable presence on Earth. The poems have been arranged to flit into and out of each other, rather than chronologically or alphabetically. The title, "On a Bat's Wing" is not an accidental misquotation of Shakespeare. There is quite a tradition of turning the bat's back of Ariel's song into a wing, and it was felt that a bat's wing would give this anthology a better, springier send-off into the world.

I started collecting poems for this anthology in 1998. In the search I was greatly encouraged by Janet Woodhead of the Cumberland Bat Group, Dr. Clemency Fisher of the Liverpool Museum, Conor Kelleher, Anne Flower, Patty Briggs, and the staff of the Bat Conservation Trust. Throughout I have had the support of my live-in bat worker, my wife, Hetty, and the essential Jenny Swann and Ross Bradshaw of Five Leaves Publications who were bold enough to take on the project. And for the delightful illustrations, Edward Lear and Carri Swann apart, my thanks to Emily Faccini. Nor must I forget the many publishers and poets who have waived royalties or heavily discounted what can be a burdensome first charge on the costs of an eccentric anthology. Everyone who has helped to get the bat on the wing will enjoy the flight.

Michael Baron

From **The Tempest**
Act 5 Scene 1

William Shakespeare

Ariel: Where the bee sucks, there suck I
In a cowslip's bell I lie;
There I couch, when owls do cry.
On the bat's back I do fly
After sunset merrily:
Merrily, merrily, shall I live now
Under the blossom that hangs on the bough.

A Lecture Upon the Bat

Catriona O'Reilly

of the species *Pipistrellus pipistrellus*.
Matchstick-sized, from the stumps of their tails
to the tips of their noses. On reversible toes,
dangling from gables like folded umbrellas.

Some of them live for thirty years
and die dangling. They hang on
like the leaves they pretended to be,
then like dying leaves turn dry.

*Suspicions amongst thoughts are like bats
amongst birds,* Francis Bacon writes,
they fly ever by twilight. But commonsense,
not sixth sense, makes them forage at night.

For the art of bat-pressing is not dead.
Inside numberless books, like tiny black flowers,
lie flattened bats. Even Shakespeare
was a keen bat-fowler, or so it's said.

In medieval beast books
extract of bat was a much-prized
depilator. *Reremice be blind as mice,
and lick powder and suck*

*oil out of lamps, and be most cold
of kind, therefore the blood
of a reremouse, nointed upon the legs,
suffereth not the hair to grow again.*

And how toothsome is fruit-bat soup
when boiled in the pot for an hour!
Small wonder then that the Mandarin
for both 'happiness' and 'bat' is 'fu'.

Bats have had a bad press.
Yet they snaffle bugs by the thousand
and carefully clean their babies' faces.
Their lives are quieter than this

bat lore would have us believe.
Bats overhead on frangible wings,
piping ultrasonic vespers. Bats
utterly wrapped up in themselves.

Bats' Ultrasound

Les Murray

Sleeping-bagged in a duplex wing
with fleas, in rock-cleft or building
radar bats are darkness in miniature,
their whole face one tufty crinkled ear
with weak eyes, fine teeth bared to sing.

Few are vampires. None flit through the mirror.
Where they flutter at evening's a queer
tonal hunting zone above highest C.
Insect prey at the peak of our hearing
drone re to their detailing tee:

ah, eyrie-ire, aero hour, eh?
O'er our ur-area (our era aye
ere your raw row) we air our array,
err, yaw, row wry — aura our orrery,
Our eerie ü our ray, our arrow.

A rare ear, our aery Yahweh.

The Bats

Matthew Sweeney

The bats live in the old television aerials.
I hear them above me at night, and sometimes
one will blunder through the broken window,
glancing off me or the bulb, his sonar gone.

Since the hot weather, the parks are clay.
It's good to be up here, on the 13th floor
as the wind dips no lower, and when it rains
the two basins I leave on the roof get filled.

I'm clean, I drink, and I've a net for birds.
The lift broke last year so I don't get down
to the street much, and I don't have strength to
fight the market crowds for State rations.

From here I see the city, and the hills beyond
where I went often when the buses ran
though I try not to think of the dead years,
dead from the day they took the telephone.

If I could vote now I'd head the queue
but it's as likely as hearing a bat speak.
A million X's would have stopped their march
but who can loudly say he saw it coming?

I open the door to no one, I make no sound.
Ignore them: they may leave you alone.
I still have my books that I saved to read
and the bulb still comes on from ten to twelve.

Up on the roof at midday I sit in the shade
of a chimney, and I drink the breeze
while the bats hang from the aerials, immune
to the heat, to the unnatural height, to me.

I think, then, of the bats as companions.
There is one I watch more than the rest —
already I cross the roof to touch his head,
when he moves in his sleep I back away.

Down below I stay close to the window
and pluck my wrens in the afternoon
then hang them from the ex-telephone wire
while I snitch my four hours of sleep.

The Year of the Bat, 1986

Menna Elfyn
Translated by Gillian Clarke

Between virus-weather and summer
        there came
the sound of intruders
with a knock-knock
        on my door.
A woman from the holiday home — our house's twin —
seeking rescue — from bats.

Love thy neighbour as thyself
        and I found myself standing
in her kitchen
        watching a bat
snare light like radar,
        the two-inch nails of its wings
tapping the party-walls,
        while below an old woman
crouched behind the wings
        of her open black umbrella.

Birds of a feather fly
        and I walked straight
across the picture and opened the window.
That simple act set free for good the fear
of two breeds for each other.

Who said bats were blind
and how can a beast know
       what it is to trespass?
Yet I wish I had insisted,
       'Come, live in my roof-space'
for I too hang upside-down
keeping my Welsh in the dark.
Sometimes a door opens
and I'm caught in the act
       of living innocently
where I don't belong,

and the night I watched you
       I saw in the crack between worlds
that the time will come,
       'The Year of the Welsh',
when visitors will come tiptoe
and from afar will watch us — almost extinct.

Yet, next day, how grateful
the two women from the city
for their rescue from the Draculas
of the wild west...!

And because I took the part
       of humankind
and drove you, wild thing, from the house,
       I offer my excuse:
At least you can fly.

My Affair with the Bat

Victoria Field

You seldom made eye contact so I stared
Unobserved at your *tragus*, that fleshy spike
In your extra-large ears pulsing sonar and clicking,
Locating you as it dislocated me.

I offered only fruit juice and nectar,
Thinking it sufficient and sweet
But you sank your teeth deep into my neck,
Drinking me as we danced.

Even so, I couldn't sustain you,
Aztec Lord of the Underworld, you needed
Several hundred innocent insects each day,
More bodies than mine.

I thought I'd shed you, shaken you off
With your sticky-tongued friends
No more erratic swishing and swooping all night
And shitting in belfries by day,

But all that Summer you haunted me.
I'd find you under the floorboards
Hanging from the shower curtain
Every crevice contained you —

Even the vase with *his* roses,
Yellow and pure like the sun —
You, unwanted familiar, dark bird of the Devil.

Iaith Fyw
(Living Language)

Stevie Krayer

Up in the deep litter
inside my head
newborn language
is being catlicked
into life.

Words hum and enter
waveringly, dance
to each other.
Honey drips from the beams;
I catch it on my tongue.

Even at night,
umbrella-winged
phrases flit about
or hang upside-down
from my clothes.

Batsville

Graham Mort

One night reading Raymond Chandler alone
in her apartment, she found a bat floating
face-down in the toilet bowl then called me,
the phone narking at my shell-like.

More Harpicide than homicide, she cracked,
adding that lacking a bat-slice she'd fished
it from the pan, dried it on a windowsill until
it twitched alive, each moment of resurrection
inching it from light.

But blind to love, ignoring her, shimmying side
ways, a dame in broken heels reverse-casing
the joint then clinging to the wall outside: a
sad suicide-stunter but no bored french-fry
munching crowd yelling *Jump, goddammit,
jump*!

It left in its own good time, its wings turning
their creased pages, the plot fumbled and
thickening, so that she wondered what it was
she'd just read and whether she'd understood
a single word, asking me *Will it be alright
out there*?

And me like a two-bit lawyer already working-
up its alibi from death, a cover-story to fool
her blind: unerring radar, navigational stunts,
a hunch of pure hope for that airborne prince
of darkness it was surely curtains for

this time.

Bat

Chris Preddle

A bat had died in the airing cupboard.
We found it when we were clearing out last month
from the house in Sancton. Unable to escape, when it died
it was preserved like a dried prune in the warmth.

The desiccated anatomy is still perfect: mainsail
ears, dinosaur head, the digits and membranes
of the wings, the radii, ribcage, feet, claws and tail.
It's less than thumbsize, perhaps a Daubenton's.

You would measure its weight
in apothecaries' grains. A fragment of papyrus
recovered from sand, it's difficult to handle, difficult to
    make out
the meaning of, like so many human occurrences.

I'm reminded of bog bodies, the cone-brown skins
of those put to death for a sacrifice
or punishment or some social difference.
They have re-emerged from the peat and the collective
    unconscious.

We keep the bat on tissues
in a small cardboard box on a shelf by the bed,
the bed we have made up with linen pillowcases
and bright cotton sheets from the airing cupboard.

The Bat

Michael Longley

We returned to the empty ballroom
And found a bat demented there, quite
Out of its mind, flashing round and round
Where earlier the dancers had moved.

We opened a window and shouted
To jam the signals and, so we thought,
Inspire a tangent in the tired skull,
A swerve, a saving miscalculation.

We had come to make love secretly
Without disturbance or obstacle,
And fell like shadows across the bat's
Singlemindedness, sheer insanity.

I told you of the blind snake that thrives
In total darkness by eating bats,
Of centuries measured in bat droppings,
The light bones that fall out of the air.

You called it a sky-mouse and described
Long fingers, anaesthetising teeth,
How it clung to the night by its thumbs,
And suggested that we leave it there.

Suspended between floor and ceiling
It would continue in our absence
And drop exhausted, a full stop
At the centre of the ballroom floor.

9 Willow Street

Ted Hughes

Willow Street, poetical address.
Number nine, even better. It confirmed
We had to have it. We got it.
A tower of the Muses. Freed from school
For the first time in your life, this was the cage
Your freedom flew to — a view of the Charles River
And Cambridge beyond it. Over my table
I covered the windows with brown paper,
Pushed ear-plugs in on my inflamed nerves
And sank. In the other room,
Perched up in the glare, on the cliff-edge,
You hammered your new Hermes,
Your Panic Bird chipping at the old egg,
While I rolled in my sack, with my lumber,
Along the bottom of the Charles. We huddled. Me
In my black sack striking sulphur matches
To find the eyes of Jung's nigredo. You
In a paralysis of terror-flutters
I hardly understood. I folded
Black wings round you, wings of the blackness
That enclosed me, rocking me, infantile,
And enclosed you with me. And your heart
Jumped at your ribs, you gasped for air.
You grabbed for the world,
For straws, for your morning coffee — anything
To get airborne. My bubbles
Wobbled upwards and burst emptily
In the reverberations of the turbines
Home and College had assembled in you,

That thundered the parquet
And shook you to tremblings. Your day
Was twenty-four rungs of a fire-escape
Hanging in ghastly swirls, over nothing,
Reaching up towards nothing.
What an airy Hell!
                    Boston clanged
All its atoms below, through all its circles
Between Harvard and Scollay Square. Alone
Either of us might have met with a life.
Siamese-twinned, each of us festering
A unique soul-sepsis for the other,
Each of us was the stake
Impaling the other. We struggled
Quietly through the streets, affirming each other,
Dream-maimed and dream-blind.
                              Your typewriter,
Your alarm clock, your new sentence
Tortured you, a cruelty computer
Of agony niceties, daily afresh —
Every letter a needle, as in Kafka.
While I, like a poltergeist fog,
Hung on you, fed on you — heavy, drugged
With your nightmares and terrors. Inside your Bell Jar
I was like a mannikin in your eyeball.
What happened casually remains —
Strobes of a hallucinating fever
In some heaving dimension of chemical horror.
Our only escape was into arms
That reached upwards or reached downwards
And rolled us all night eastward with each other

Over the bottom, in the muddy current.
What a waste!
What did our spectre-blinded searching reach
Or wake to, that was worth it?

                              Happiness

Appeared — momentary,
Peered in at your window
Like a wild migrant, an oriole,
A tanager, a humming-bird — pure American,
Blown scraps of the continent's freedom —
But off course and gone
Before we could identify it.

It took me a dizzy moment to make out
Something under the chestnuts, struggling
On a path of the Common, down near the Swan-boats.
What looked like a slug, black, soft, wrinkled,
Was wrestling, somehow, with the fallen
Brown, crumpled lobe of a chestnut leaf.
Suddenly, plainly, it was a bat.
A bat fallen out of its tree
Mid-afternoon. A sick bat? I stooped
Thinking I'd lift it again to tree-bark safety.
It reared up on its elbows and snarled at me,
A raving hyena, the size of a sparrow,
Its whole face peeled in a snarl, fangs tiny.
I tried to snatch it up by the shoulders
But it spun, like a fighter, behind its snarl.

A crowd collected, entertained to watch me
Fight a bat on Boston Common. Finally
I had to give it my finger.
Let the bite lock. Then, cradling it,
Gently lifted it and offered it up
To the wall of chestnut bark. It released me
And scuttled upwards backwards, face downwards,
A rearguard snarl, triumphant, contorted,
Vanishing upwards into where it had come from.

At home I looked at the blood, and remembered:
American bats have rabies. How could Fate
Stage a scenario so symbolic
Without having secreted the tragedy ending
And the ironic death? It confirmed
The myth we had sleepwalked into: death.
This was the bat-light we were living in: death.

Pipistrelle

Gillian Clarke

Dusk unwinds its spool
among the stems of plum-trees.
Subliminal messenger
on the screen of evening.
A night-glance as day cools
on the house-walls.

We love what we can't see,
illegible freehand
fills every inch of the page.
We sit after midnight
till the ashes cool
and the bottle's empty.

This one, in a box, mouse
the size of my thumb in its furs
and sepia webs of silk
a small foreboding,
the psalms of its veins
on bible paper,

like a rose I spread once in a book
till you could read your future
in the fine print.

Vocations

Geoffrey Hill

While friends defected, you stayed and were sure,
fervent in reason, watchful of each name:
a signet-seal's unostentatious gem
gleams against walnut on the escritoire,

focus of reckoning and judicious prayer.
This is the durable covenant, a room
quietly furnished with stuff of martyrdom,
lit by the flowers and moths from your own shire,

by silvery vistas frothed with convolvulus —
radiance of dreams hardly to be denied.
The twittering pipistrelle, so strange and close,

plucks its curt flight through the moist eventide;
the children thread among old avenues
of snowberries, clear-calling as they fade.

The Bat and the Two Weasels

La Fontaine, from Aesop
Translated by Edward Marsh

Bat, intent upon her evening quest,
Butted head-first into a Weasel's nest;
And she, who bore the Mice an ancient grudge,
Flew to devour th' unwelcome guest.
"What, so you dare," she cried, "to show your face,
After the wrongs I've suffered from your race?
Ain't you a mouse? Speak truth! If I'm a judge,
You are — or else no weasel I."
"Not so," was our poor friend's reply,
"To such estate I have no claim.
A mouse? Some tatler has traduced my name.
Thanks to the Father of All Things,
I am a bird — you see my wings.
Long live the tribe that cleaves the sky!"
The Weasel found her reasoning good,
And set her free to roam the wood.
Next day, my feckless heroine
Approached, upon a fresh excursion,
Another Weasel's home, and blundered in.
This time, 'twas birds that were the pet aversion:
Here was her life at stake once more!
The long-nosed housewife, scurrying to the door,
Was just about to crunch her as a bird,
When she protested — it was too absurd!
"I, pass for such? You can't have looked at me.

What is the one unfailing sign
To tell a bird? The feathers — where are mine?
I am a mouse: long live the Rats,
And Jupiter confound the Cats!"
By this resourceful repartee
Once more she gained her liberty.

'Tis thus the wise, when faction threats,
Will sport reversible rosettes,
And tactfully the changes ring
On *Up the League!* And *Up the King!*

Say What You Are

for Michael & Hetty

Christopher Pilling

And Noah said: The wrong answer could bar you
       from entering the Ark: What are you?

The two bats claimed they were neither cat nor mouse.
You're not welcome in our solar-panelled house,
Said Noah and prepared to throw them out....

But Shem said: The wrong answer could bar you
       from entering the Ark: What are you?

The two bats claimed they were neither man nor beast.
You're not welcome at our Integrated Molecular Feast,
    said Shem
And raised his fork.

But Ham said: The wrong answer could bar you
       from entering the Ark: What are you?

The two bats claimed they were neither bird nor fish.
You're not in our supersatellite dish, are you? Keep clear
    or... said Ham,
You'll spoil our reception.

But Japheth said: The wrong answer could bar you
       from entering the Ark: What are you?

The two bats claimed they were neither dodo nor quagga.
You're not welcome in our New World Zoo, said Japheth
— He was chief keeper and vet but couldn't cope with
    Extinct.

But Noah's wife said: The wrong answer could bar you
        from entering the Ark: What are you?

The two bats claimed they were neither whale nor shark.
You're not welcome in this Theme Park Ark, or our life,
Said Noah's wife, sharpening her kitchen knife.

But a voice came from above:
    Don't let your answer come too pat, said a raven,
    And don't pull a face —
    It's no disgrace looking like that.
And a taxidermist nodded.

A voice from below decks called up: The wrong answer
    could bar you
        from entering the Ark: What are you?

The two bats claimed they were neither hound nor hare.
The taxidermist, for that's who it was, didn't care,
Introduced himself, said nothing but Welcome,
        He wasn't bluffing....

They didn't know what a taxidermist was
And looked forward to the stuffing.

Sixteen Dogs, Cats, Rats and Bats

Geoffrey Grigson

Sixteen dogs and sixteen cats
Went chasing after sixteen rats.
The sixteen rats were full of fear
And wished that they were bats, in air.
No sooner wished than so they were,
The sixteen rats were sixteen bats
Safe above all dogs and cats,
And to and fro, and fro and to,
About the sky at night they flew,
Leaving the sixteen cats to howl
And the sixteen dogs to growl.

They did not like it in the sky
Where all their food was moth and fly,
They had no cheese, they licked no butter,
They slept behind a leaky gutter
Upside down as all bats sleep,
And now they wished once more to creep
In rat-shape round a rubbish heap.

No sooner wished than they were down
Dragging their tails around the town
And sixteen dogs and sixteen cats
At once appeared and ate those rats.

MORAL: Better be a living bat
Than line the stomach of a cat.

Bats

George MacBeth

have no accidents. They loop
their incredible horse-shoe
loops, dead-stop

on air-brakes,
road-safe on
squeaks: racketeering

their SOS noise in a
jai-alai
bat-jam

of collapsed umbrellas, a
Chancery Lane
of avoided

collisions, all in a
cave without lights: then
hung

happy, a snore
of strap-hangers
undergrounding

without an *Evening*
Standard between them
to the common Waterloo

that awaits bats, like
all beasts, then
off now, zoom!

Man, you can't even
hear them; bats,
are they?

The Bat

Frank Jacobs

Bats are creepy; bats are scary;
Bats do not seem sanitary;
Bats in dismal caves keep cozy;
Bats remind us of Lugosi;
Bats have webby wings that fold up;
Bats from ceilings hang down rolled up;
Bats when flying undismayed are;
Bats are careful; bats use radar;
Bats at night-time at their best are;
Bats by Batman unimpressed are!

Rat-bat

Roy Fisher

Please be quiet. You can't always hear
us, but we can certainly
hear you. It's painful,
I make this gesture so that you can know
what system means. No,
we don't pee up our own noses
when we're asleep. We're
organised for that, too. The entire
Typing P… the entire Resource Interface
is making, through me, exactly
the same statement. Please listen.

Sonar

Angela Leighton

Dusk flushes the last light out   and sprouts
a bat,   flibbertigibbet, twitchy as nerves,
a phoning flicker, radar-singer.   And airy

as air, quick as a wink,   this flittermouse,
chamois leather,   dodges back, and back,
in a flap.   It calls each fact, maps the sound

of each obstacle thing.   Busy musician,
twittering wavelengths,   you make quick shapes
in your ears, you hear   the size of everything.

And we, in the half-dark,   sonar-sounded,
are noted also,   modulated
like stones and trees and walls.   We're all

ear-shapes, sound-ghosts,   plucked frequencies
drawn from the shadows.   This is the stuff
you sing by, steer by,   audible, avoidable.

Listen. Don't move.   Our dialled echoes
are pitched exactly   in another perspective,
tapped like rumours,   quickly transmitted.

Tiny busker, mathematician,   your flight
shirks matter lightly,   puzzles our physics.
Take your bearings.   Keep your distance.

This phoned world comes over and over,   micro-
soundings in the ear's soundboard.   Listen close.
It's thick with music,   answeringly tuned.

Silky Oak

Martin Langford

All night, the flying fox carnival plays
in the great golden cone of the tree.
Beatings and shudderings, as they land
and re-land; scrapings, and rubbings of skin.
They cannot hang still,
but must stretch-tension-hug to the next,
and the next, spill of glories. And the veins
of their throats must be dancing: high-pitched
and shameless miaows of amazement; a warping
of thin, metal echoes; a layered erotics of chatter
with scoldings and fades — *This tree's*
a night sky of nectar, a field of furred combs!
They smash their way through in excitement:
tossing behind them a carpet of alphabet parts —
a porridge of used claims and meanings —
stripped, left to rot, in the bright stare of day.

The Bats

Tinker Mather

Fine feet creep in
to comb my hair,
small mouths plant quiet
blind kisses on my skin.

Clinging to my chin they lift
their leather nostrils to find out
where my breath comes from
and where it goes.

They follow it up my nose. Sliding shut
their wings they press along the passageways,
carrying away on their caramel fur
the mess inside my head.

My mouth opens in surprise
and they fly out in a cloud
of efficient lithe bodies
and a rush of fetid air.

I sleep all night in my clean swept skull
as they stream like demon mice
above me, dusting off the debris
against the indigo sky.

The Bat of Totality

Penelope Shuttle

Sombre eclipse, more Scriabin than Chopin
Tenebrous eclipse, more Bruckner than Ravel

A drag of silver over the sea's sky:
rain or moon shadow?

No one can tell,
yet when the brakes of the cosmic car tighten

to a standstill
we feel this unseen eclipse in our bones,

brains, hearts, genes,
as evident as if we saw it through solar filters —

Eclipse more inner than outer —

until the swoop of total dark,
longest two minutes of my life,

including any two minutes
of the hours I was in labour.

Near Helston, a lone bat woke,
skedaddled across a friend's field,

maybe thinking,
where are my mothers, my fathers and my brothers,
my sons and my daughters,

my kin and my matrikin,
all my affines?

Bats

Jacob Polley

Tonight, above the river where we sit,
    we imagine the water's electric.

Cut it off. Let the riverbed
    be stripped to its musculature
of mud and eels, its shelves of green-haired stones:
    we want to see what every stone

hides at the centre of its head.
    And from the earth, among the minerals,
from the caves where the cereals sleep,
    come thoughts hardly thoughts, barely notions

or beliefs, to flutter at the light's edge.
    They have fur, and skin like an ear's.
The whole night is how they listen
    to our minds in the dark, full of stars.

Karlsbad Caverns

Ted Hughes

We had seen the bats in the Karlsbad caves,
Thick as shaggy soot in chimneys
Bigger than cathedrals. We'd made ourselves dots

On the horizon of their complete world
And their exclusive lives.
Presumably the whole lot were happy —

So happy they didn't know they were happy,
They were so busy with it, so full of it,
Clinging upside down in their stone heavens.

Then we checked our watches. The vanguard bats,
To the minute, started to flicker and whirl
In the giant mouth of the cavern

That was our amphitheatre, where they were the drama.
A flickering few thickened to a million
Till critical boiling mass tore free of the magnet

Under the earth. The bats began to hurl out —
Spill out, smoke out, billow out,
For half an hour was it, an upward torrent

Of various millions of bats. A smoky dragon
Out of a key-hole in earth,
A great sky-snake writhing away southwards

Towards the Rio Grande
Where every night they caught their tons of insects —
Five tons, somebody said.

And that was how it should be.
As every night for how many million years?
A clockwork, perfected like their radar.

We weren't sure whether to stay that night or go.
We were where we had never been in our lives.
Visitors — visiting even ourselves.

The bats were part of the sun's machinery,
Connected to the machinery of the flowers
By the machinery of insects. The bats' meaning

Oiled the unfailing logic of the earth.
Cosmic requirement — on the wings of a goblin.
A rebuke to our flutter of half-participation.

Thoughts like that were stirring, when somebody yelled.
The sky-dragon of bats was making a knot.
'They're coming back!'
                              We stared and we saw,

Through the bats, a mushrooming range
Of top-heavy thunderheads, their shutters flashing
Over the Rio Grande. The bats had a problem.

Wings above their heads like folding umbrellas
They dived out of the height
Straight back into the cave — the whole cloud,

The vast ragged body of the genie
Pouring back into the phial. All over the South
The storm flashed and crawled like a war.

Those bats had their eyes open. Unlike us,
They knew how, and when, to detach themselves
From the love that moves the sun and the other stars.

Bat

Sue Hubbard

Between sweat-damp sheets
I lie listening to the hum
of the fan watching
the fat chunk of American moon
hanging above the distant Adirondacks,
in the blue-black night
phosphorescent beyond the rose garden.
My naked body in the heavy heat
accustoming itself to the low breathing
of the narrow bed, to my own touch
hauling myself in like a hand reaching
for someone drowning in deep water,
when as if from the edge of another world —
a flap of inky rag
in the melon moonlight —
it flits in through some forgotten
crack in a drawn screen to appear
silent at the end of my bed
dragging its sooty blacks,
its umbrella wings,
propelling its furry face,
that prick-eared mouse-mask
into my airless room.
I had wanted
skin, muscles, nerves
a heart between these hot sheets,
not this assault from beyond
the fringe of lamp-light;
this gigolo of shadows,
turning my stomach inside out
as he quickens towards me,
tiny white teeth and black cloak,
dark as fresh blood.

The Present

Michael Laskey

Poking about in the garage
for tacks to patch up the flapping
felt on the roof I can't not
notice the bat-box. Last summer
he made it. That's six supine months
it's lain on the shelf, all my passing
thoughts swerving unerringly off.
Yet such a cinch to put up:
the holes ready drilled; the required
nails still taped on, like a spray
of slender grey flowers for a wedding;
and certainly somewhere indoors
the Nature Conservancy Council
pamphlet he lent me on bats,
advice on choosing a site.
So thoroughly green — he's used nothing
but off-cuts of untreated wood —
and so diligent, it makes me sick
of myself, my sloth, this life-
size mock-up of my head with its knots,
its slit, tight lid and misplaced
dark void that might have provided
for pipistrelles, say, or noctules.

A Bat in a Box

Robert Nye

The long cold cracked and I walked in the cracks
To pay the rent for the first time in weeks
And pick our post up from the farm on the top road.

That done — "Has your son," said the farmer's wife,
"Ever seen a bat in a box? I have one
You could take back to show him."

And I imagined how a bat in a box
Would beat its bloodshot wings, and comb itself
With greedy claws, and eat up flies and beetles;

And how, when hanging by the wing-hooks, it
Would sleep, long ears tucked under, as if cloaked:
And how its tameness might in fact confound me.

I did not take it, back down through the snow
To show my son.
                    Why did I not do so?

To tell you, I would have to undo winter,
Thaw my bare heart and waste its bitterness,
Losing the wry frost with some deeper drifts.

A bat,
        in a box.
                    Just think of it.

Protected Species

Susan Wicks

My parents' papers lie round me
bundled in boxes, the lids dotted
with the droppings of bats, the names
faded, too faint for a stranger's eye
to interpret. I pull, and the perished bands
snap into dust, a grey sheet blisters
with flying fragments. *Joy darling:*
in the roof his circling voice
transmits its high-pitched signal
to her voice. My parents' wartime letters,
starred with small explosions, have flown
great distances, their words blanching
on the page, their steady messages
bringing the world back
to an attic where protected species
hang upside-down, flexing
their claws in a dream of darkness,
shaking their skinny wings.

The Bat

Ted Hughes

The beggarly Bat, a cut out, scattily
Begs at the lamp's light
A bright moth-mote.

What wraps his shivers?
Scraps of moon cloth
Snatched off cold rivers.

Scissored bits
Of the moon's fashion-crazes
Are his disguises
And wrap up his fits —

For the jittery bat's
Determined to burst
Into day, like the sun.

But he never gets past
The dawn's black posts.

As long as night lasts
The shuttlecock Bat
Is battered about
By the rackets of ghosts.

Pipistrelles

Kathleen Jamie

In the centre of the sheep-field
a stand of Douglas firs
hold between them, tenderly,
a tall enclosure like a vase.

How could we have missed it
before today — never have seen
this clear, translucent vessel
tinted like citrine?

What we noticed were pipistrelles:
cinder-like, friable, flickering
the place hained by trees
till the air seemed to quicken

and the bats were a single
edgy intelligence, testing their idea
for a new form
which unfolded and cohered

before our eyes. The world's
mind is such interstices;
cells charging with light of day —
is that what they were telling us?

But they vanished, suddenly,
before we'd understood,
and the trees grew in a circle,
elegant and mute.

from **Childhood**

John Clare

On summer eves with wild delight
We bawled the bat to spy
Who in the "I spy" dusky light
Shrieked loud and flickered bye
& up we tossed our shuttlecocks
& tried to hit the moon
& wondered bats should flye so long
& they come down so soon.

Darkness

Mike Johnson

I
am
the
bats'
friend
nightly
I clothe
the world
in deepest
shadows and
silences yet
creatures who
can use shadow
and silence fly
far and wide fly
here and there to
swish swoop swish!

swish swoop swish!
here and there to
far and wide fly
and silence fly
can use shadow
creatures who
silences yet
shadows and
in deepest
the world
I clothe
nightly
friend
bats'
the
am
I

The Bat

Ogden Nash

Myself, I rather like the bat,
It's not a mouse, it's not a rat.
It has no feathers, yet has wings,
It's quite inaudible when it sings.
It zigzags through the evening air
And never lands on ladies' hair,
A fact of which men spend their lives
Attempting to convince their wives.

Are Umbrellas Really Bats?

For Jenny Swann

John Lucas

In case of rain
avoid the strain
of touting an umbrella;
to shield your head
unfurl instead
a pipistrelle — a
large one will best suit,
though no need for the fruit
battiness of the monster flying fox —
on whom a pox.

Carri Swann

Uncle Bram

Roger McGough

Uncle Bram
a bat-catcher of distinction
scorned the use of
battraps, batnets and bat poison.
"Newfangled nonsense,"
he would scoff, and off
he would go
to hang upside down
in belfries for days on end
in the hope of snatching
one of the little bastards.

Bats

John Tranter

In a freezing attic somewhere in Prague
a hungry songwriter invents Sincerity, but alas,
too early. A decade later, a popular singer,
struck by the intimacy a microphone fakes,
invents a way of sobbing in time to the music —
earnest little hearts are wrecked
from San José to Surbiton. The angelic
choirs, should they be tempted to rebel,

would they hit on a trick so lucrative? Clouds
of butterflies reassure us: we are so much more
serious, and intelligent — think of rockets, and
the invention of dentistry and napalm. Sincerity?
It will take a Poet Laureate to turn it to profitable use.
Bats circle the Old City, low and silent.

Local Legend

John Ashbery

Arriving late at the opera one night
I ran into Dr. Gradus ad Parnassum hastening down the
    marble stair,
swan-like. "I wouldn't bother if I was you," he confided.
"It's a Verdi work written before he was born.
True, his version of the Faust legend is unique:
Faust tempts Mephistopheles to come up with something
besides the same old shit. Finally, at his wits' end, the devil
urges Valentine to take his place, promising him big rewards,
this side of Old Smoky. Then, wouldn't you know,
    Gretchen gets involved.
They decide to make it into a harassment case. No sooner
does Faust hit the street than the breeze waffles his brow,
he can't say where he came from, or if he ever had a youth
to be tempted back into."
                The bats arrived. It was their moment.
Twenty million bats fly out of an astonishingly low culvert
every night, in season. I kid you not. After a cursory swoop
or two, they all fly back in. It all happens in a matter of
minutes, seconds, almost. Which reminds me, have you
    chosen your second?
Mephisto wants you to use this foil. It works better.
No, there's nothing wrong with it.

Hours later I stood with the good doctor
in a snow-encrusted orchard. He urged the value
of mustard plasters on me. "See, it makes sense."
Yet we both knew they are poisonous in some climates,
though only if taken in minute quantities.

See you again, old thing.

Dream Song '63 (extract)

John Berryman

Bats have no bankers and they do not drink
and cannot be arrested and pay no tax
and, in general, bats have it made.
Henry for joining the human race is *bats*
known to be so, by few them who think,
out of the cave.

Instead of the cave! Ah lovely-chilly, dark,
ur-moist his cousins hang in hundreds or swerve
with personal radar,
crisisless, kid. Instead of the cave? I serve,
inside, my blind term. Filthy four-foot lights
reflect on the whites of our eyes.

He then salutes for sixty years of it
just now a one of valour and insights,
a theatrical man,
O scholar & Legionnaire who as quickly might
have killed as cast you. *Olé!* Stormed with years
he tranquil commands and appears.

Off the Ground

The Triforium Gallery, Winchester Cathedral

Matthew Francis

   If you could fly
  this might be the place for it,
in the colonnades of air over the heads
   of the walkers,

   like bats unhooked
  from their hanging villages
to explore the pinnacles of the chantries,
   the chapel caves,

   the high corners
  out of the reach of dusters,
the web-blinded windows and ledges gritted
   with dried-up flies,

   a house so tall
  flying things are at home here;
but we who have to climb stairs can cling on, too,
   half off the ground,

   Saints and angels,
  struck from their old perches, rest
in the gallery around us, and a Bible
   lies near at hand,

   with dancing room
  between the pages for
the red, blue and gold figures with pointed toes
   and open wings.

Mind

Richard Wilbur

Mind in its purest play is like some bat
that beats about in caverns all alone,
contriving by a kind of senseless wit
not to conclude against a wall of stone.

It has no need to falter or explore;
darkly it knows what obstacles are there,
and so may weave and flutter, dip and soar
in perfect courses through the blackest air.

And has this simile a like perfection?
The mind is like a bat. Precisely. Save
that in the very happiest intellection
a graceful error may correct the cave.

Enigmas Part III

Roy Fuller

What is it like to be a bat? It seems
An expert suggests that their experience
Is much like ours. And yes, sometimes the sense

Comes in of flying through the dusk of dreams
Or hanging upside down in dreamless sleep.
And consciousness itself's the strangest thing —

The retina's screen or radar system of
The animal, to which the otherwise
Indifferent atoms have evolved through chance.

— So most maintain, believing time alone
Has made the variously coloured eye,
And patent stow-away umbrella wing.

Life

Jo Shapcott

My life as a bat
is for hearing
the world.

If I pitch it right
I can hear
just where you are.

If I pitch it right
I can hear inside your body:
the state of your health,

and more, I can hear
into your mind.
Bat death is not listening.

My life as a frog
is for touching
other things.

I'm very moist
so I don't get stuck
in the water.

I'm very moist
so I can cling
onto your back

for three days
and nights.
Frog death is separation.

My life as an iguana
is for tasting
everything.

My tongue is very fast
because the flavour
of the air is so subtle.

It's long enough
to surprise
the smallest piece of you

from extremely far away.
Iguana death is a closed mouth.

Bats

Geraldine Green

I lie and watch them flit and sift the air
like black flour in a thunderstorm,
their hail-rained wings, torn shreds
of velvet ribbon, slice the breath
I breathe.

These bats, gone in a quick moist moment
of dusk, flicking grey mist from leather wings,
their slick mouse bodies, ears pointed
fox nosed things, you bats!
I lie and watch.

All But Blind

Walter de la Mare

All but blind
   In his chambered hole
Gropes for worms
   The four-clawed Mole.

All but blind
   In the evening sky
The hooded Bat
   Twirls softly by.

All but blind
   In the burning day
The Barn-Owl blunders
   On her way.

And blind as are
   These three to me,
So, blind to Some-One
   I must be.

B was a Bat

Edward Lear

B was a bat,
Who slept all the day,
And fluttered about,
When the sun went away.
      b!
   Brown little Bat.

The Power of Words

Steve Krayer

All day I devote myself to testing
the power conferred by words. I make
my wishes known with *Ball Water Foodge
Carry, Nana! Me do!* My grownups
usually respond satisfactorily —
even better than pressed phone buttons.

Sometimes I find I must
reject, having required. But I try to
provide some explanation:
Too hotsh! No nice! Hard!
Now and then, though, it's just
NO! That ought to be enough, really.

When I teach them new words
they can be slow. I am patient,
repeat *Matoes? matoes?* until
they stop looking puzzled and asking
what's wrong with my toes. Don't they know
it's lunchtime?

But after night falls, there is something
I haven't got a name for.
Bats? I suggest. And we leave
what is lit, and warm, and known,
making do with a blanket and
my grandpa's arms for walls.

I try *Dark!* and am silent
for a little while. Then I propose
Stars. Moon. And again, *Bats.* I can't
usually bear it for long. *Back house.*
I've noticed that Nana, for all
her hoard of years and poet-words
can only echo me. *Yes, darling — bats!*

The Bat

Theodore Roethke

By day the bat is cousin to the mouse.
He likes the attic of an ageing house.

His fingers make a hat about his head.
His pulse beat is so slow we think him dead.

He loops in crazy figures half the night
Among the trees that face the corner light.

But when he brushes up against a screen,
We are afraid of what our eyes have seen:

For something is amiss or out of place
When mice with wings can wear a human face.

The Bat

Emily Dickinson

The Bat is dun, with wrinkled Wings —
Like fallow Article —
And not a song pervade his Lips —
Or none perceptible.

His small Umbrella quaintly halved
Describing in the Air
An Arc alike inscrutable
Elate Philosopher.

Deputed from what Firmament —
Of what Astute Abode —
Empowered with what Malignity
Auspiciously withheld —

To his adroit Creator
Ascribe no less the praise —
Beneficent, believe me,
His Eccentricities —

The Bat

Ruth Pitter

Lightless, unholy, eldritch thing,
Whose murky and erratic wing
Swoops so sickeningly, and whose
Aspect to the female Muse
Is a demon's, made of stuff
Like tattered, sooty waterproof,
Looking dirty, clammy, cold.

Wicked, poisonous, and old:
I have maligned thee! ... for the Cat
Lately caught a little bat,
Seized it softly, bore it in.
On the carpet, dark as sin
In the lamplight, painfully
It limped about, and could not fly.

Even fear must yield to love,
And pity makes the depths to move.
Though sick with horror, I must stoop,
Grasp it gently, take it up,
And carry it, and place it where
It could resume the twilight air.

Strange revelation! warm as milk,
Clean as a flower, smooth as silk!
O what a piteous face appears,
What great fine thin translucent ears!
What chestnut down and crepey wings,
Finer than any lady's things —
And O a little one that clings!

Warm, clean, and lovely, though not fair,
And burdened with a mother's care:
Go hunt the hurtful fly, and bear
My blessing to your kind in air.

Man and Bat

D.H. Lawrence

When I went into my room, at mid-morning,
Say ten o'clock...
My room, a crash-box over that great stone rattle
The Via de' Bardi...

When I went into my room at mid-morning
Why? ... a bird!

A bird
Flying round the room in insane circles.

In insane circles!
... A bat!

A disgusting bat
At mid-morning! ...

Out! Go out!

Round and round and round
With a twitchy, nervous, intolerable flight,
And a neurasthenic lunge,
And an impure frenzy;
A bat, big as a swallow!

Out, out of my room!

The venetian shutters I push wide
To the free, calm upper air;
Loop back the curtains ...

Now out, out from my room!

So to drive him out, flicking with my white handkerchief:
  Go!
But he will not.

Round and round and round
In an impure haste,
Fumbling, a beast in air,
And stumbling, lunging and touching the walls, the
    bell-wires
About my room!

Always refusing to go out into the air
Above that crash-gulf of the Via de' Bardi,
Yet blind with frenzy, with cluttered fear.

At last he swerved into the window bay,
But blew back, as if an incoming wind blew him in again.
A strong inrushing wind.

And round and round and round!
Blundering more insane, and leaping, in throbs, to clutch at
    a corner
At a wire, at a bell-rope:
On and on, watched relentless by me, round and round in
    my room,
Round and round and dithering with tiredness and
    haste and increasing delirium
Flicker-splashing round my room.

I would not let him rest;
Not one instant cleave, cling like a blot with his breast to the
    wall
In an obscure corner.
Not an instant!

I flicked him on,
Trying to drive him through the window.

Again he swerved into the window bay
And I ran forward, to frighten him forth.
But he rose, and from a terror worse than me he flew
    past me
Back into my room, and round, round, round in my room
Clutch, cleave, stagger,
Dropping about the air
Getting tired.

Something seemed to blow him back from the window
Every time he swerved at it;
Back on a strange parabola, then round, round, dizzy
    in my room.

He *could* not go out;
I also realised ...
It was the light of day which he could not enter,
Any more than I could enter the white-hot door of a blast-
    furnace.

He could not plunge into the daylight that streamed at the
    window.
It was asking too much of his nature.

Worse even than the hideous terror of me with my
    handkerchief
Saying: *Out, go out! ...*
Was the horror of white daylight in the window!

So I switched on the electric light, thinking: *Now
The outside will seem brown ...*
But no.
The outside did not seem brown.
And he did not mind the yellow electric light.

Silent!
He was having a silent rest.
But never!
Not in my room.

Round and round and round
Near the ceiling as if in a web
Staggering;
Plunging, falling out of the web,
Broken in heaviness,
Lunging blindly,
Heavier;
And clutching, clutching for one second's pause,
Always, as if for one drop of rest,
One little drop.

And I!
Never, I say ...
Go out!

Flying slower,
Seeming to stumble, to fall in air.
Blind-weary.

Yet never able to pass the whiteness of light into freedom ...
A bird would have dashed through, come what might.

Fall, sink, lurch, and round and round
Flicker, flicker-heavy;
Even wings heavy:
And cleave in a high corner for a second, like a clot, also a
    prayer.

But no.
Out, you beast.

Till he fell in a corner, palpitating, spent.
And there, a clot, he squatted and looked at me.
With sticking-out, bead-berry eyes, black,
And improper derisive ears,
And shut wings
And brown, furry body.

Brown, nut-brown, fine fur!
But it might as well have been hair on a spider: thing
With long, black-paper ears.

So, a dilemma!
He squatted there like something unclean.

No, he must not squat, nor hang, obscene, in my room!

Yet nothing on earth will give him courage to pass the
   sweet fire of day.

What then?
Hit him and kill him and throw him away?

Nay,
I didn't create him.
Let the God that created him be responsible for his death ...
Only, in the bright day, I will not have this clot in my room.

Let the God who is maker of bats watch with them in their
   unclean corners ...
I admit a God in every crevice,
But not bats in my room;
Nor the God of bats, while the sun shines.

So out, out you brute! ...
And he lunged, flight-heavy, away from me, sideways,
   a sghembo!

And round and round and round my room, a clot with wings
Impure even in weariness.

Wings dark skinny and flapping the air,
Lost their flicker.
Spent.

He fell again with a little thud
Near the curtain on the floor.
And there lay.

Ah, death, death,
You are no solution!
Bats must be bats.

Only life has a way out.
And the human soul is fated to wide-eyed responsibility
In life.

So I picked him up in a flannel jacket,
Well covered, lest he should bite me.
For I would have had to kill him if he'd bitten me, the
        impure one …
And he hardly stirred in my hand, muffled up.

Hastily, I shook him out of the window.

And away he went!
Fear craven in his tail.
Great haste, and straight, almost bird straight above the
        Via de' Bardi.
Above that crash-gulf of exploding whips,
Towards the Borgo San Jacopo.

And now, at evening, as he flickers over the river
Dipping with petty triumphant flight, and tittering over
        the sun's departure,
I believe he chirps, pipistrello, seeing me here on this
Terrace writing:
There he sits, the long loud one!
But I am greater than he …
I escaped him …

In Memoriam R.G.C.

D.J. Enright

What (hardly his best) I best remember — not
The essays on the Great Reviews in *Scrutiny*
But the matter of the little bat
That we happened on, hurt and twitching weakly
At the bottom of a staircase in the quad,
Like a creature struck by fine distinctions.

Someone should put it out of its misery
As educated people would agree,
But we were all so bloody tender
(And I had been reading *Dracula*) —
Then he came by, for some our supervisor,
Soon to join the Friends' Ambulance Unit.

Not famous as a friend of Chiroptera
But famously anxious and kind-hearted,
Older and wiser, a College officer.
He pulled a face as we led him to the spot.

One purblind peep, and the bat arose hangdog
And teetered off. It recognised authority.
Like Lazarus! we said: which grieved his modesty.

Zoo Bats

John Updike

In the Central Park Zoo, just past the ants,
being televised by tiny cameras,
the bats flutter and swoop in a glassed-in gloom.
You don't see bats this close up very often.

Yet they are hard to see, too quick, too faint,
and their shapes disagree with the eyes —
appall us, really, though we approach and peer
determined not to be appalled, to be liberal and just

toward this creature that is, after all,
remarkably successful, if quietly so.
One seventh of all mammalian species
are Chiroptera, and their mortality rate

is low, their predators no problem, and
their child-rearing habits more constant than ours.
Who begrudges them their diet of grubs?
Their digestions are rapid, to keep themselves light.

For all this Fourierism, this favorable press,
these bats in the flesh are worse than we dreamed;
if we dreamed of them often, we would swap
such sleep for death, its featureless white glare.

They are shapeless in flight and in repose —
Small broken umbrellas that grab the air
like brown-gloved skeletal hands, and latch
their sticky feet to a roost with a vile

tenacity, and tremblingly hang; or else
they drop to a ledge like a sudden deposit
of excrement, shit out of nowhere, a
product of this intestinal gray gloom.

No doubt they have dear faces — with nose-flaps,
some of them, to aid echolocation,
and snouts, like the hog-nosed bat of Thailand,
small as a bumblebee. The common bat

that haunts our mauve suburban twilights with
its airborne evening meal — connect the dots —
weighs one third of an ounce, or less. How minor
a mass for so disquieting a shadow!

Perhaps to fly with webbed and lengthened fingers
sits worse, with nature, than to do it with
thoracic chitin-scales or feathered arms.
A bird in a new shape, a fish of the sky;

a bat, a squeaking face between a pair
of agitated hands, that's all. I once
was at a party when a bat broke in.
It dipped from room to room as people screamed.

The host at last opened a door, and out
it went. To make his teary daughter laugh,
I said, "It looked like this," and did a face —
a-squint, stretch-mouthed. She laughed and said, "It did!"

We see them better than we know, like the
subliminal bits on television.
They are subconscious, bats, and bubble up
like prejudices. Another time, one night,

I saw a bat sail like a black flung stone
behind my stepson's head. He and my wife
reacted violently, and, slamming doors,
delegated me to be the bat

eliminator. Trapped, I crept upstairs,
through hall and bedroom (nothing there) into
the bathroom where, all fearful of its flying
Dracula-fanged and rabid at my face,

I found it hanging, folded, to a towel.
Resigned and upside down, the bat had sensibly
amid our panic put itself to sleep.
Stealthy as a parent, I wrapped it gently up;

it chirruped, exerting a questioning pressure
back through the towel like the throb of a watch.
Up, window. Up, screen. I gave the bat back
to the night like a cup of water to the sea.

Bat Ode (Downtown Columbus, Rush Hour)

Jeredith Merrin

Dead, of course, but with soft,
egg-sized black body and
scalloped, coal-satin wings —
so pretty, it was hard

not to be happy to
have the rare city sight
of it. Hyper-real
(the way death always is),

and mildly exotic;
a sidewalk *frisson*, breaking middle-aged boredom.
(Everyone, everyone

becomes predictable —
especially the young
rebels, so timidly
indistinguishable,

and the "mature" beige ones:
alike in their terror
of appearing foolish
at all costs, at great cost,

inestimable cost.)
The bat was new, intact.
Heart flutter suddenly
stopped, dropped to the pavement.

O Delicately Veined,
Neat Eared, Night Wandering.
Neither epiphanic
lark, nightingale, nor rook.

A Bat Is Born
From **The Bat Poet**

Randall Jarrell

A bat is born
Naked and blind and pale.
His mother makes a pocket of her tail
And catches him. He clings to her long fur
By his thumbs and toes and teeth.
And then the mother dances through the night
Doubling and looping, soaring, somersaulting —
Her baby hangs on underneath.
All night, in happiness, she hunts and flies.
Her high sharp cries
Like shining needlepoints of sound
Go out into the night and, echoing back,
Tell her what they have touched.
She hears how far it is, how big it is,
Which way it's going:
She lives by hearing.
The mother eats the moths and gnats she catches
In full flight; in full flight
The mother drinks the water of the pond
She skims across. Her baby hangs on tight.
Her baby drinks the milk she makes him
In moonlight or starlight, in mid-air.
Their single shadow, printed on the moon
Or fluttering across the stars,
Whirls on all night; at daybreak
The tired mother flaps home to her rafter.
The others are all there.
They hang themselves up by their toes,
They wrap themselves in their brown wings.
Bunched upside down, they sleep in air.
Their sharp ears, their sharp teeth, their
        quick sharp faces
Are dull and slow and mild.
All the bright day, as the mother sleeps,
She folds her wings about her sleeping child.

The Absence of Bats

Elizabeth Barrett

We spend a week of dusks hunting for bats,
pointing your box at half-lit skies,
turning the volume up — ending our days
on the banks of rivers and reservoirs,
visiting ramshackle friends with roosts.
There is a help-line to fix kits that refuse
to work but, you say, what we have,
perhaps, is an absence of bats.

We need to feed the box with things
inaudible, to offer it short wavelengths,
other ultrasounds, to find a testing
frequency high enough to stir its circuit
board and convert silence to a lower pitch —
the stream of warbles, clonks and clicks
that we would hear if there were bats.

So we test the detector with ultrasonic ideas.
We click our fingers, jangle keys,
drop pins. We scrape our shoes on gravel;
try dog-whistles, the rustle of a nylon jacket.
We whisper into the oblong box, trip and twist
our tongues on consonants which tick and hiss.
Through all of this the box stays silent.

Our son too is silent. Like a black box
he absorbs noise. Our words are dropped
stones spiralling to echo in a black well,
the repeated ripple of our voices fading,
stilled. Mostly the audible world sinks
without trace in him. But today, as we scrunch
and crumple an ultrasonic crisp packet,

he turns and runs and suddenly the box fizzes
and splutters. At first I am convinced that it
is him — grab the box and chase our son
around the house, scanning his body in,
trying to convert his silence, decipher him.
The Detector is keeping quiet again.
How can you be sure, I ask, that an absence
of sound means there aren't any bats?

*

Later, I look up from my book — tell you
that the long-eared bat is seldom detected:
it only ever whispers its call; flies high,
twists and turns among trees; hears,
faultlessly, the insect and the leaf.
Upstairs our son is sleeping. He's tucked his ears
beneath his wings to twirl his wordless pirouettes.
I kneel to feel the whisper of his mothy breath.

A Bat on the Road

A batlike soul waking to consciousness of itself in darkness and secrecy and loneliness

Seamus Heaney

You would hoist an old hat on the tines of a fork
and trawl the mouth of the bridge for the slight
bat-thump and flutter. Skinny downy webs,

babynails clawing the sweatband... But don't
bring it down, don't break its flight again,
don't deny it; this time let it go free.

Follow its bat-flap under the stone bridge,
under the Midland and Scottish Railway
and lose it there in the dark.

Next thing it shadows moonslicked laurels
or skims the lapped net on a tennis court.
Next thing it's ahead of you in the road.

What are you after? You keep swerving off,
flying blind over ashpits and netting wire;
invited by the brush of a word like *peignoir*,

rustles and glimpses, shot silk, the stealth of floods
So close to me I could hear her breathing
and there by the lighted window behind trees

it hangs in creepers matting the brickwork
and now it's a wet leaf blowing in the drive,
now soft-deckled, shadow-convolvulus

by the White Gates. Who would have thought it? At the
    White Gates
She let them do whatever they liked. Cling there
as long as you want. There is nothing to hide.

89

Learning About Bats

Pat Borthwick

What is a mammal?
How can you tell which is the long-eared bat?
We learnt much that night
walking between the Douglas Firs
and round by the ponds where we halted.
Our warden waved life-size celluloid cut-outs,
the sky not yet quite the right shade of grey.

Their fingers are long and joined by twin membranes.
Only the thumb ends in a claw.
You slipped your hand inside my zip-up,
smoothly homed in on a nipple while
the expert explained where pipistrelles live,
how they hunt nocturnal insects like moths.
You'd set a jittery moth in my cave.

They moisten their claws with their lips and tongue
to oil their elastic wings. Once punctured, they often die.
It's much darker now.
A huge red moon rolls from the horizon
chased by Mars. The party in front moves on,
follows the sloping path through more trees
where a man high on a ladder opens a box.

Bats' flight paths are straight, except in pursuit of food.
They capture winged insects the rate of two every second.
Then they come, skittering out of the sky,
giddy, zig-zagging between branches and stars,
between the shrieks of our group. Torches
try to hitch on their chase and can't. Needles
twitch in red vectors, echolocators chirp.

Bats mate once a year by the full Autumn moon
although often the egg stays unfertilised until Spring.
You seem surprised when I unpick
the seam of your fur with my teeth, climb
through your rafters on wrists and hind feet,
to hang from the pulsing moon of your heart.
Taste your fingers. They're thick with my milk.

Bats

Vicki Feaver

Only at night, the noisy nursery wakes:
the mothers who've taken over the space
in the roof returning from insect-gathering
flights. I can hear the flutter
as they squeeze in under the eaves,
the twittering, chirruping, squeaking,
of milk-sucking, carnivorous throats.
In the day, you wouldn't know they were there,
except for a smell, made up of bits of smells
I thought I'd forgotten — a hamster cage,
grandma's fusty feather mattress,
the iron reek of a birth room.
I ought to award them honour.
I could take a broom and sweep
their hanging bodies from the beams.
Once, one flew into our bedroom, spinning
above our heads, wings like the contraptions
Leonardo strapped to the backs of men
pattering against ceiling and walls,
stirring nightmares of claws
in the hair, teeth in the neck.
It settled on top of the wardrobe.
I climbed up, saw, in the half dark,
pointed ears move. It was a baby,
just learnt to fly. I wanted it
to be mine: to feed it like my daughter
feeds my granddaughter on the choicest
delicacies, to go out into the wet fields
and search for beetles and crane-flies
and moths, to make it a doll's
soft cot, to rear it with the man
who pulled a sock over his hand

and gently lifted it up, launching it
through the window, returning to the bed
where care is not for the flesh of our flesh
but flesh itself, hands, tongues, the body's
tenderest morsels, offered from each
to each, shared like food.

The Bat

Edith Sitwell

Castellated, tall
From battlements fall
Shades on heroic
Lonely grass,
Where the moonlight's echoes die and pass,
Near the rustic boorish,
Fustian Moorish
Castle wall of the ultimate Shade,
With his cloak castellated as that wall, afraid,
The mountebank doctor,
The old stage quack,
Where decoy-duck dust
Began to clack,
Watched Heliogabalusene the Bat
In his furred cloak hang head down from the flat
Wall, cling to what is convenient,
Lenient.
"If you hang upside down with squeaking shrill,
you will see dust, lust, and the will to kill,
and life is a matter of which way falls
your tufted turreted Shade near these walls.
For muttering guttering shadow will plan
If you're ruined wall, or pygmy man,"
Said Heliogabalusene, "or a pig,
Or the empty Caesar in tall periwig."
And the mountebank doctor,
The old stage quack,
Spread out a black membraned wing of his cloak
And his shuffling footsteps seem to choke,
Near the Castle wall of the ultimate Shade
Where decoy-duck dust
Quacks, clacks, afraid.

Lady Dracula

George MacBeth

Lady Dracula
Flies into my mind,
I hear her wings whistle
An' her teeth grind.

> *Lady Dracula*
> *With long black hair,*
> *Lady Dracula*
> *With red fangs bare*

Lady Dracula
Is hungry for blood,
She digs deep in
An' she sucks real good.

> *Lady Dracula*
> *With long black hair,*
> *Lady Dracula*
> *With red fangs bare*

Lady Dracula
Was once alive,
She drinks men's blood
From nine to five.

> *Lady Dracula*
> *With long black hair,*
> *Lady Dracula*
> *With red fangs bare*

When the sun rises,
She goes to bed,
Lady Dracula:
You'll find her dead.

> *Lady Dracula*
> *With long black hair,*
> *Lady Dracula*
> *With red fangs bare*

The Bats' Plea

Elizabeth Jennings

Ignore the stories which say
We shall fly to and tangle your hair,
That you are wise if you dread
Our mouse-like bodies, the way
Our wings fan out and spread
In gloom,in dusty air.

Eagles are lucky to be
Thought of in terms of light
And glory. Half-bird,half-beast,
We're an anomaly.
But, clinging to darkness we rest
And, like stars, belong to the night.

They Say of Bats...

John Kinsella

They can make you fear all creatures:
scare tactics, the bat that will tangle
in your hair after sunset, need to be hacked
out with scissors, claws and bones
and membranes knotted down, veins
plugging into the skull, filling
follicles and biting thought-patterns
with alliteration; the short distance
between air and skin layer that touches
the hemisphere of skull, asymptotic,
is the black transparency of a batwing
stretched against dull luminance of a town
or light burning deep below the rim
of horizon, a faint memory or gesture,
sometimes filled with spite, the day
not quite going right; and the teeth
they'll call rabid where no rabies
has been reported, an agility without sight
that makes a corrupt diagnosis;
and fear mythologises like "trinkets
dangling from an elderly woman's
once glamorous neck", these miniature
beasts always threatening to grow larger
than the sky will take, come down
out of cavities in trees and hillocks,
festeringly social in their own communities,
yet, we're warned, smothering ours,
quick to die in your hair,
get under your skin.

Assault & Battery

Carole Baldock

In a tree in Transylvania
Hang two hungry bats, full of dismay.
They haven't had a bite to eat;
Their stomachs grumble, and so do they.

Up comes the Scouse bat
(Bit dim, hasn't seen the light),
"Ar eh lads, what's up wit youse?"
"Not von neeble, the entire night."

"Ve could even manage a well-done steak,
Mit eggs, sunny side up."
"Doan' worry, I'll 'ave a good luk round,
Bring youse back summat to sup."

Sure enough, in five minutes, he returns,
Absolutely covered in blood.
Tells them both to follow him
And flies to the end of the wood.

"D'yet see dat great big tree out der?"
"Of course ve do, you daft... bat"
And the Scouse bat says very crossly,
"Well, I wish I bloody 'ad!"

ratbat

Caroline Carver

de swooping ratbat
got no working eyes

but move like speeding airplane

ratbat done sleep
all upside down

but don get muddle in de head

scuffle squeak
in silly high pitch voice

but no one laughing

I tink if ratbat come in here
wait for see doctor

de ladies say he tangle up de hair
an run out shrieking

Daubenton's Bats

Gill Nicholson

After the swallows fly off
silence condenses over the tarn,
hangs there as the sun gravitates
towards the wooded hill.

Reflections of oak and ash give black depths
to the secret current of the feeder
except where final flares
silver the mid-stream runway

an air corridor suddenly alive
to the flicker and whirl
of water bats, the spokes
of their half-umbrella wings

spread wide as a man's hand-span.
Noiselessly these swallows of the dusk
skim for flies and midges
curve and loop in flight,

dip, kiss the glassy surface,
each mirror image
a lover
in silhouette.

Bat Samba

it was their moment — John Ashbery

Tamar Yoseloff

If they find you at home, they'll skitter
towards your lights, their tiny squeaks
audible only to the dog, who circles his tail
in torment. Do they want your love
or is it something more tangible? The safety
of your house? The roof over your head?
Once in, they want to thank you, naturally,
so they flap with delight, like the dead
doing the samba as you try to sleep.

You want to kill them — but there are laws,
fines, imprisonment, the universal scorn
of bat fanciers. They know this and flaunt it
every opportunity they get. You are past caring.
You would feel no guilt if there was one less
butt-ugly creature — you, who give to charity,
who love dogs and cats, even mice,
but these monsters have been put on earth
to try you, to see how far your compassion goes.

Your compassion stops here. They have entered
your dreams, with their foul bat breath,
beady blind eyes. You conjure them into vampires
hunkering down in your bed for the night.
Only a matter of time until you wake to find
your teeth have sharpened to fangs, your body
is covered with wiry hair and your back
has sprouted wings — brown, veined, hideous.
It's just as well you can't see.

From **Little Verses for Very Little Children**

William Allingham

> Bat, bat, come under my hat,
> And I'll give you a slice of bacon;
> And when I bake
> I'll give you a cake
> If I am not mistaken.

A Bat

Dorothy Cowlin

For me they were always
small packages of delight
coming out of the blue June evening,
flickering shadows,
silent as moths
but swifter and more wayward:
repetitive syllables
in the long spell of summer.

Today, a workman,
called to arrest the crumbling
of our local dark ruin, stood by the tower,
a small creature clinging to his
T-shirt.

Only a little larger than a moth,
its dark fur
puffed in the wind like smoke.
Wings hung like silk
of a furled doll's umbrella.
Its pen-nib mouth
opened and closed without a sound
more piteous for that.

Gently I touched it:
there seemed no substance
nothing but fur
and the fine grey fabric
of its folded wings.

The Fairy Bell

*A renegade poet, having taken to journalism for more
money, is rebuked by his Muse in the form of an old
gentleman; he cuts her throat.*

Stevie Smith

A dismal bell hung in the belfry
And clanged a dismal tune
And back and forth the bats did fly
Wherever there was room.

He seemed melancholy but a reasonable creature,
Yet I could see about his hat as it were this belfry steeple.

The Agony through which I go,
He said, is something you ought to know
And something that you will know too
When I have finished telling you.

He took my hand, I could not choose but stand,
Perhaps for his own sake he should not have done this?
Yet I thought Death was the best prize, if he won this.

Oh, the sad music of the backward and forth
Flying of the bats, pleading for worth,
But in this perhaps again I was wrong —
That there was for him some enjoyment in their song?

It is done now and I cannot trouble to rue it,
I took his gullet in my hand and with my knife cut through it.

But still in my head I sometimes hear the soft tune
Of the belfry bats moaning to find more room
And the ding-dong of that imaginary sound
Is as grateful as a fairy bell tolling by waters drowned.

From **The Feast of Bacchus
(The Metamorphoses, Ovid)**

Translated by *Arthur Golding*

Alonely Minyas' daughters bent of wilfulness, with working
Quite out of time to break the feast, are in their houses
    lurking:
And thee do fall to spinning yarn or weaving in the frame,
And keep their maidens to their work; of which one pleasant
    dame
As she with nimble hand did draw her slender thread and
    fine,
Said: "While that others idly do serve the God of Wine,
Let us that serve a better saint, Minerva, find some talk
To ease our labour while our hands about our profit walk.
And for to make the time seem short, let each of us recite —
As everybody's turn shall come — some tale that may
    delight."
Her saying liked the rest so well that all consent therein,
And thereupon they pray that first the eldest would begin.

Their tales did end and Minyas' daughters still their
    business ply
In spite of Bacchus whose high feast they break
    contemptuously.
When on the sudden, seeing nought, they heard about
    them round
Of tubbish timbrels perfectly a hoarse and jarring sound,
With shreaming shawms and jingling bells and furthermore
    they felt
A scent of saffron and of myrrh that very hotly smelt.
And (which a man would ill believe) the web they had begun
Immediately waxed fresh and green , the flax the which
    they spun
Did flourish full of ivy leaves, and part thereof did run

Abroad in vines. The thread itself in branches forth
     did spring
Young burgeons full of clustered grapes their distaffs forth
     did bring,
And as the web they wrought was dyed a deep dark purple
     hue,
Even so upon the painted grapes the selfsame colour grew
The day was spent and now was come the time which
     neither night
Nor day, but middle bound of both, a man may term of right.
The house at sudden seemed to shake, and all about it shine
With burning lamps, and glittering fires to flash before
     their eyen.
And likenesses of ugly beasts with ghastful noises yelled.
For fear whereof in smoky holes the sisters were compelled
To hide their heads, one here and there another, for to shun
The glistering light. And while they thus in corners blindly
     run,
Upon their pretty limbs a fine crisp film there goes,
And slender fins instead of hands their shortened arms
     enclose,
But how they lost their former shape of certainty to know
The darkness would not suffer them. No feathers on
     them grow.
And when they go about to speak they make but little sound,
According as their bodies give, bewailing their despite
By chirping shrilly to themselves. In houses they delight
And not in woods; detesting day they flitter towards night:
Wherethrough they of the evening late in Latin take
     their name,
And we in English language bats or reremice call the same.

Echolocation

John Altringham

Seeing in sound, the bat sings a solo
Echoes enriched in the reflections of the night
Detailing the dark, defining its world
A cappella performed with the wind
The familiar sound of woodland and water
A minimalist music.

The echo of a maybug modulated by movement
Its wings glinting, a beating beacon
A promise of food in the shifting soundscape

The night insects, unsuspecting mirrors
Betray their presence to the hunter
The night singer, seeing its way in sound

Vol de Nuit

for Hetty

Michael Baron

Sharing the joy, the look on your face,
the softening of the wrinkle
under your left eye —
you'd said weighing
trapped in a muslin bag.
the tiniest bundle in the world —
"four grammes, flesh and fur"
then parted wings in a gentle fan.
Snarl of pointy teeth, our bat launched
from the table like an angry hurdler
facing a last jump, flew to the sink.
Fifty seconds of excited flight,
the kitchen a grand circle, surprised;
one refugee soprano pipistrelle
saved from a market dustbin.
And flew again into night.
Windows casements
opening onto air and tree;
and unsuspecting midges
dancing their last wild waltz.

Echoes

for S.A.

Grevel Lindop

Each evening, once the children were in bed,
I'd climb the garden wall and scramble off
its damp, bouldery top into hogweed and nettles
round the end of the building; then among moths and
    headstones
to the porch, where I could ease the latch up, gently
swing the door open and hang back from the threshold
to watch a blue-grey slice of window ahead
for the scrap of black that suddenly flicked across,
brief as a trick of the fading light, but again
and again, becoming real though no less strange
with repetition. Stepping into the nave,
I would hear a small continuous rumpling noise
like someone shaking and shaking a soft leather glove
that refused to come right side out, until the waft
of air hit my cheek as a pipistrelle completed
its lap and circled my head before diving away
down the length of the church. I'd strain my ears
    for something
beyond that dull flutter: a chirp, an echo, some key-
signature to the labyrinth of harmonics
the bat must be threading, the sibilant cat's-cradle
of tremors pitched from the hammerbeam roof, the layered
darkness marbled with intersecting coils
of notes fanned from its diapason of squawks
by diffraction around the sandstone pillars, the floor
a stone pool whose reflective surface glinted
fugitive barks and cadenzas, except where I
was planted, a plume of muffling vapours, lit
by the flare of a curious moth. I could distinguish
nothing, though as I walked to the door my shoe-soles

released, I suppose, scuffed cymbal-crashes that burst
like surf up the walls, their last resonance dissolving
into the throat of the bell as I latched the door
with its figured bass of iron.
          Later that summer
we rented another house six miles away
down the coast, near a field where a noctule hunted
      at sunset,
ranging slowly across the sky — a small
black bird, it seemed, until it swooped and the frantic
flutter of wings came clear, a labour of flying
quite different from the hurtling glide of the swifts
with which sometimes it hunted. Taking a path
where corn-marigold and scabious straggled on
at the dusty margins of the wind-combed grasscrop,
I was almost afraid, the first time, of two people
inhumanly still, and watching me from the slope
at the western end of the field. I stared them out
and strode on over the clods as if I knew
where I was going and who owned the place
until I could see their rubber-glove hands, their faces
of swathed blue polythene sack. Standing beside them
to watch the bat sweep overhead, across
rags and strips of apricot cloud, I could hear
all at once, the *pew, pep-pew* of its cry, a metallic
pizzicato twitched from the sky, and sensed
how the field with its drifts and spirals of air, its crop
of faintly seething insects, might be mapped
in a trawl of twilight echoes. Up at the gate
near the cliff-edge I turned and waved back at the house —
though I couldn't tell if you saw, the windows were merely
tiles of flame set into the grey slate wall —
a ritual I repeated each evening we stayed there.
The bat persisted too, even after the field
had been scalped and baled for silage, and the scarecrows
leant in a distant corner, their heads together
as if comparing notes, somehow attuned
to subtleties I had already missed.

I'll Go So Far

Christopher Pilling

I only know the pipistrelle
that "little squeaky beast"
because my daughter found one dead
by Crummock (*crooked*)
and sent it to be identified.

I only know the things it eats
because the *Collins Mammal Field Guide*
by David (*darling*)
 and Priscilla (*previous*)
lists the likely creatures

       — as many as three thousand in a night
       all swallowed while in flight....

And I can say with pride:
I know — but cannot hide
that my knowledge is what you'd call secondhand
which *bona fide* bat men wouldn't understand.

I'm like any bat —
If I feel the cold
I go inside.
I pursue derivations.
I'm prepared to take the scholar's view.

Finding a dead bat though is something new.
I suggested what my daughter could do.
Reading up in a book is ok too.

I see bat in German is *Fledermaus* (flying mouse),
in Italian it's *pipistrello*,
in French it's *chauve-souris* (bald mouse).
Oh no!

I'll watch bats briefly at any time of day
swooping and looping the loop
but when midnight strikes
or I strike it lucky at cheese-pared feasts
with down-to-earth *grisettes*,
those nice grey mice,
I'm through
with bald ones, whiskered ones and the likes:
all *"little squeaky beasts"*.

So bats adieu!

The Bat

Jane Kenyon

I was reading about rationalism,
the kind of thing we do up north
in early winter, where the sun
leaves work for the day at 4:15.
Maybe the world is intelligible
to the rational mind;
and maybe we light the lamps at dusk
for nothing....

Then I heard wings overhead.

The cats and I chased the bat
in circles — living room, kitchen,
pantry, kitchen, living room....
At every turn it evaded us

like the identity of the third person
in the Trinity: the one
who spoke through the prophets,
the one who astounded Mary
by suddenly coming near.

Fruit Bat Colony by Day

Les Murray

High above its gloom
this forest is all hung
with head-down ginger bats
like big leather bees.

In sun to stay drowsy
daylong in slow dangle
chi-chi as monkeys
they blow on sad tin horns,
glide, nurture babies, sleep,
waiting for their real lives.

Contributors' Notes

William Allingham (1824-1889): "To The Bat" from "Little Verses for Little Children" was included in the *Oxford Book of Nursery Rhymes* (ed. Opie, OUP, 1955). Allingham was an Irish man of letters and poet. *The Poems of William Allingham* was published by OUP in 1967.

John Ashbery: "Local Legend" from *Chinese Whispers* (Carcanet, 2003). His 26th collection is *A Wordly Country* (Carcanet, 2007). Pulitzer Prize winner 1976. His *Selected Prose 1953-2003* was published by Carcanet in 2005.
BY PERMISSION OF CARCANET.

John Altringham: "Echolocation" is first published here. He is Professor of Biomechanics at Leeds University and author of *British Bats* (Collins New Naturalist Series, 2003), and of the preface to the anthology.
BY PERMISSION OF THE AUTHOR.

Carole Baldock: "Assault & Battery" is first published here. She is editor of the international literary magazine *Orbis*. Her first collection *Give Me Where to Stand* was published by Headland in 2007. Other books include *How to Raise Confident Children*.
BY PERMISSION OF THE AUTHOR

Michael Baron: "Vol de Nuit" is first published here. He is co-editor of *Wordsworth and The Famous Lorton Yew Tree* (LDFLHS) 2004, and the editor of this anthology.

Elizabeth Barrett: "The Absence of Bats" is from *The Bat Detector* (Wrecking Ball Press, 2005). Her first collection was *Walking on Tiptoe* (Staple, 1998). She has been co-editor of poetry magazine *Staple* and is a lecturer in English at Sheffield Hallam University.
BY PERMISSION OF THE AUTHOR.

John Berryman (1914-1972): "Dream Song '63" is from *Dream Songs* (Faber, 1969). His *Collected Poems* was published by Faber in 1990.
BY PERMISSION OF FABER.

Pat Borthwick: "Learning About Bats" is first published here. She lives on a farm in North Yorkshire. Her first collection, *Swim,* was published by Mudfog in 2005.
BY PERMISSION OF THE AUTHOR.

Caroline Carver: "Ratbat" from *Bone Fishing* (Peterloo, 2007). Her first collection was *Jingharzi and Me* published in 2000. She was the winner of the 1998 National Poetry Competition.
BY PERMISSION OF THE AUTHOR AND PETERLOO POETRY.

John Clare (1793-1864): An extract from "Childhood". His first book, *Poems: Descriptions of Rural Life and Scenery*, was published in 1820. Various editions of his poems were published in the twentieth century including *The Shepherd's Calendar* (OUP) in 1964 and *Selected Poems* (Dent) in 1965.

Gillian Clarke: "Pipistrelle" from *Letting in the Rumour* (Carcanet, 1989). She has published five poetry collections, including *Collected Poems* (Carcanet, 1997) and *Making Beds for the Dead* (Carcanet, 2004).
BY PERMISSION OF CARCANET.

Dorothy Cowlin: "The Bat" from *The Dalesman* magazine. She has published novels, biographies for children, and poems in magazines.
BY PERMISSION OF THE AUTHOR.

Emily Dickinson (1830-1886): "The Bat". Save for six poems, her poetry was found and published after her death. After several editions, the complete *Collected Poems* was published in 1995.

Menna Elfyn: "The Year of The Bat" (also in Welsh) from *Eucalyptus* (Gomer, 2007). Her *Collected Poems* will be published by Bloodaxe Books in 2007. She is editor of *The Bloodaxe Book of Modern Welsh Poetry*.
BY PERMISSION OF THE AUTHOR AND GOMER.

D.J. Enright (1920-2002): "In Memoriam R.G.C." from *Under the Circumstances* (OUP, 1991) reprinted in *Collected Poems, 1948-1998* (OUP), published 1998. He published numerous collections of verse, as well as novels, children's books, and edited *The Oxford Book of Contemporary Verse, 1945-80*. Awarded the Queens Gold Medal for Poetry in 1981.
BY PERMISSION OF WATSON, LITTLE LTD.

Vicki Feaver: "Bats" from *The Book of Blood* (Cape, 2006), which was short-listed for the 2007 T.S. Eliot Prize, and for the 2006 Forward Prize — her third collection after *Close Relatives* (1981) and *The Handless Maiden* (1994).
BY PERMISSION OF THE AUTHOR AND RANDOM HOUSE GROUP.

Victoria Field: "My Affair With the Bat" from *Olga's Kitchen* (Fal, 2004). Her last collection was *Many Waters* (Fal, 2006).
BY PERMISSION OF THE AUTHOR AND FAL.

Roy Fisher: "ratbat" from "Figures from Anansi Company" in *The Long and the Short Of It, Poems 1955-2005* (Bloodaxe, 2005). He has published twelve poetry collections.
BY PERMISSION OF BLOODAXE BOOKS.

Matthew Francis: "Off The Ground" from *Dragons* (Faber, 2005). His other collections are *Blizzards* (Faber, 1996) and *Whereabouts* (Rufus Books, 2005). He is the editor of the *New Collected Poems of W.S. Graham* (2004) and teaches creative writing at the University of Wales, Aberystwyth.
BY PERMISSION OF THE AUTHOR AND FABER.

Roy Fuller (1912-1991): "Enigmas Part III" is from *Last Poems* (Andre Deutsch, 1993). He was Professor of Poetry at

Oxford University. His *New and Collected Poems* was published by Andre Deutsch in 1985.

BY PERMISSION OF JOHN FULLER.

Arthur Golding (1536?-1603?): from "The Feast of Bacchus" (*Ovid — Selected Works,* Dent, 1939). Poet and prolific translator; his translation of *The Metamorphoses* brought Ovid to English readers.

Geraldine Green: "Bats" is first published here. Her last collection was *Passio* (Flarestack, 2006). She teaches creative writing and is working on a third collection of poetry.

BY PERMISSION OF THE AUTHOR.

Geoffrey Grigson (1905-85): "Sixteen Dogs, Cats, Rats and Bats" from *Collected Poems — 1963-1980* (Allison and Busby, 1982). Journalist, and critic, founder of the influential New Verse 1933-1939. An advocate for popular verse, his *Book of Popular Verse* was published by Faber in 1971.

BY PERMISSION OF DAVID HIGHAM ASSOCIATES.

Seamus Heaney: "A Bat on the Road" from *Station Island* (Faber, 1984). His last collection, which won the 2007 T.S. Eliot Prize, was *District and Circle* (Faber, 2006). *Opened Ground — Collected Poems 1966-1996* was published in 1998. Seamus Heaney won the Nobel Prize for Literature in 1995.

BY PERMISSION OF THE AUTHOR AND FABER

Geoffrey Hill: "Vocations" from *Tenebrae* (Viking Deutsch, 1992). His *Collected Poems* was published in 1985, his most recent collection is *Without Title* (Penguin, 2006).

BY PERMISSION OF PENGUIN GROUP

Sue Hubbard: "Bat" from *Ghost Station* (Salt, 2004). Her first collection was *Everything Begins with Skin* (Enitharmon, 1994). The Poetry Society's first Public Art Poet. Her novel *Depth of Field* was published in 2000. A freelance critic and columnist for the *Independent*.

BY PERMISSION OF SALT.

Ted Hughes (1930-2000): "The Bat" from *Collected Animal Poems* (Faber, 1995), "9 Willow Street" and "Karlsbad Caverns" from *Birthday Letters* (Faber, 2001). Ted Hughes was Poet Laureate 1984-2000.
BY PERMISSION OF FABER.

Frank Jacobs: "The Bat": See note on page 127.

Kathleen Jamie: "Pipistrelles" from *The Tree House* (Picador, 2004), winner of the 2004 Forward Prize ©Kathleen Jamie, 2004. Her *Mr and Mrs Scotland Are Dead* (2002) covers the years 1980-1994. Travel and other non-fiction books include *Findings* (Sort Of Books, 2005).
BY PERMISSION OF PAN MACMILLAN.

Randall Jarrell (1914-1965): "A Bat Is Born" from *The Bat Poet* (illustrated by Maurice Sendak, New York, 1964) and from the *Complete Poems* (Faber, 1969). *The Bat Poet*, a children's story, is the supreme poetic and fictional homage to a bat.
BY PERMISSION OF FABER.

Elizabeth Jennings (1926-2001): "The Bats' Plea" from *A Spell of Words* (Macmillan). Her *Collected Poems* was published by Carcanet in 1987.
BY PERMISSION OF DAVID HIGHAM ASSOCIATES.

Mike Johnson: "Darkness": from *Creatures of the Night* (Beggis Books, 1993). He has a PhD in experimental writing. See note on page 127.

Jane Kenyon (1947-1983): "The Bat" from *Let Evening Come — Selected Poems 1978-1996* (Bloodaxe World Poets, 2005). This includes translations of twenty poems by Anna Akhmatova.
BY PERMISSION OF BLOODAXE BOOKS.

John Kinsella: "They Say of Bats" from *The New Arcadia* (W.W. Norton, 2005). His last collection was *America: A Poem* (Arc, 2006). His poem "Forest Encomia of the South West" was shortlisted for the Forward Prize, 2006, Best Single Poem.
BY PERMISSION OF THE AUTHOR AND SALT.

Stevie Krayer: "Living Language" from *Questioning the Planet* (Gomer, 2005). "The Power of Words" is first published here. Her first collection was *Voices From a Burning Boat* (1997), and she is the author of a translation of Rilke's *The Book of Hours* (1995), both from the University of Salzburg Press.
BY PERMISSION OF THE AUTHOR AND GOMER.

Martin Langford: "Silky Oak" was published in *Island 106*, Spring 2006. His last collection was *Sensual Horizons* (Five Islands, 2001). In 2004 he co-edited *Ngaia* a companion volume for the Australian Poetry Festival, and in 2005 Island published his *Microtexts* a book of aphorisms and observations on poetics.
BY PERMISSION OF THE AUTHOR.

Michael Laskey: "The Present" from *The Tightrope Wedding* (Smith/Doorstop Books, 1999). His earlier collection was *In the Fruit Cage* (Smith/Doorstop Books (1997). He co-edits the poetry magazine *Smiths Knoll*, and founded the Aldeburgh Poetry Festival.
BY PERMISSION OF THE AUTHOR.

D.H. Lawrence (1885-1933): "Man and Bat" from *Complete Poems,* (London, 1964). This poem first appeared in *Birds, Beasts and Flowers* in 1923.

Edward Lear (1816-1888): "It was a Bat" from *Lear Alphabet ABC* (Constable Young Books, 1965). Another "bat" or "B" poem is on page 39 of *The Cretan Journal* of 1864 (Athens, 1984). *The Complete Nonsense and Other Verse* was published by Penguin in 2001.

Angela Leighton: "Sonar" is first published here. Her first collection was *A Cold Spell* (Shoestring Press, 2000). Shoestring will publish *Sea Level* in 2007. Professor Leighton is a Research Fellow at Trinity College, Cambridge and the author of several books on nineteenth and twentieth century poetry.
BY PERMISSION OF THE AUTHOR.

Grevel Lindop: "Echoes" from *Playing with Fire* (Carcanet 2006). He has published five verse collections, and most recently *Selected Poems* (Carcanet, 2000). Formerly a Professor of English at Manchester Victoria University, he is the biographer of Thomas De Quincey, and author of *A Literary Guide to the Lake District*.
BY PERMISSION OF THE AUTHOR AND CARCANET.

Michael Longley: "The Bat" from *Collected Poems* (Cape Poetry, 2006). T.S. Eliot Prize winner in 2000, and the Queen's Gold Medal for Poetry in 2001. A study of his poetry, *Reading Michael Longley,* was published by Bloodaxe Books in 2006.
BY PERMISSION OF THE AUTHOR AND RANDOM HOUSE GROUP.

John Lucas: "Are Umbrellas Really Bats?" is first published here. He is the founder and editor of Shoestring Press. Professor Emeritus at the Universities of Loughborough and Nottingham, he is author of scholarly and critical works, and has published eight poetry collections, the last being *Flute Music* (Smokestack Books, 2006).
BY PERMISSION OF THE AUTHOR.

George MacBeth (1932-1992): "Lady Dracula" from *Collected Poems, 1958-1982* (©George MacBeth, Hutchinson, 1989). A *Selected Poems* was published by Enitharmon in 2002. He published eighteen verse collections, also novels and children's books , and was editor of *The Faber Book of Animal Verse*.
BY PERMISSION OF SHIEL LAND ASSOCIATES LTD. ON BEHALF OF THE GEORGE MACBETH ESTATE.

Roger McGough: "Uncle Bram" from *Sporting Relations* (Penguin, 1974). Other collections from this co-founder of the "Liverpool Poets" include *Selected Poems, 1967-1987*, and *You at the Back* (Cape, 1991).
"UNCLE BRAM" ©ROGER MCGOUGH IS REPRODUCED BY PERMISSION OF PFD (WWW.PFD.CO.UK) ON BEHALF OF THE AUTHOR.

Walter de la Mare (1876-1956): "All But Blind" from *Collected Rhymes and Verses* (Faber, 1989). He published nineteen books of poems between 1902 and 1953. His poems

were in each of Sir Edward Marsh's Georgian Poetry anthologies 1912-1922. Also a novelist and short story writer. His poetry was given new life by the publication in 2006 of *Selected Poems of Walter de la Mare* (Faber) edited by Matthew Sweeney.
BY PERMISSION OF THE SOCIETY OF AUTHORS FOR THE WALTER DE LA MARE ESTATE.

(Sir) **Edward Marsh** (1872-1953): "The Bat and the Two Weasels" from Book Two of *The Fables of La Fontaine* (Heinemann, 1933). Sponsor of the "Georgian" school of poets, particularly Rupert Brooke and Siegfried Sassoon, and Walter de la Mare. He was Winston Churchill's private secretary in 1905.
BY PERMISSION OF DAVID HIGHAM ASSOCIATES.

Tinker Mather: "The Bats" from *Unsettled Idylls* (Poetry Direct, Oxford, 2005). She worked as a painter before turning to writing a decade ago.
BY PERMISSION OF THE AUTHOR.

Jeredith Merrin: "Bat Ode (Downtown Columbus, Rush Hour)" from *Bat Ode* ©The University of Chicago, 2001. Merrin's works-in-progress include a book of poems and a collection of critical essays on poets and poetry. She teaches at Ohio State University.
BY PERMISSION OF THE AUTHOR AND UNIVERSITY OF CHICAGO PRESS.

Graham Mort: "Batsville" from *A Night On The Lash* (Seren, 2004). His first collection was *Circular Breathing* (Dangeroo Press, 1997). He is Director of post-graduate studies in creative writing at Lancaster University.
BY PERMISSION OF THE AUTHOR AND SEREN.

Les Murray: "Bats' Ultra Sound" from *Translations from the Natural World* (Carcanet, 1993) and "Fruit Bat Colony By Day" from *Poems The Size of Photographs* (Carcanet, 2002). His most recent collection was *The Biplane House* (Carcanet, 2006). Won the T.S. Eliot Prize in 1996, and the Queen's Gold Medal for Poetry in 1999.
BY PERMISSION OF THE AUTHOR AND CARCANET.

Ogden Nash (1902-1971): "The Bat" from *In The Living Room*, originally in the *Saturday Evening Post* in 1952. He published fourteen collections of verse. "A playful hater of dullness like Carroll, Lear and W.S. Gilbert". In 2002 the U.S. Postal Service issued stamps of Ogden Nash and six of his short poems.
BY PERMISSION OF CURTIS BROWN LTD.

Gill Nicholson: "Daubenton's Bat" is first published here, and was a runner up for the Mirehouse Poetry Prize in 2006. Author of several plays and short stories.
BY PERMISSION OF THE AUTHOR.

Robert Nye: "A Bat In a Box" from *The Rain and the Glass: 99 Poems, New and Selected* (Greenwich Exchange, 2005)). In 1989 his poems were collected in *A Collection of Poems 1955-1988*. He has published novels and several books for children, and is a poetry reviewer and critic.
BY PERMISSION OF THE AUTHOR AND CURTIS BROWN LTD.

Catriona O'Reilly: "A Lecture on the Bat" from *The Nowhere Birds* (Bloodaxe, 2001). Her second collection, *The Sea Cabinet,* was published by Bloodaxe Books in 2006.
BY PERMISSION OF THE AUTHOR.

Chris Preddle: "Bat" was a prize winning poem in the 2001 Biscuit Poetry competition. He is currently working on a translation of Sappho's poems and fragments.
BY PERMISSION OF THE AUTHOR.

Christopher Pilling: "I'll Go So Far" and "Say What You Are" are both published here for the first time. His last collection of translations was *Love at the Full* (Flambard, 2004), and his next, *Defying Fate*, of the poet Maurice Careme, will be published by Arc in 2007. He was awarded the John Dryden Prize in 2006 for his translations of Catullus.
BY PERMISSION OF THE AUTHOR.

Ruth Pitter (1897-1992): "The Bat" from *Collected Poems* (Dufour Editions, 1969). A critical assessment of her poetry is

in *Ruth Pitter: Homage to a Poet* (Dufour Editions, 1969).
BY PERMISSION OF MARK PITTER.

Jacob Polley: "Bats" is published here for the first time. His
first collection was *The Brink* (Picador, 2003) and the second
Little Gods (Picador, 2006). His poem "Cheapjack" was short-
listed for the 2006 Forward Best Single Poem.

Theodore Roethke (1905-1963): "The Bat" from *Collected
Poems* (Faber 1985). He published seven collections, the last
being *The Far Field* in 1964.
BY PERMISSION OF FABER.

William Shakespeare (1564-1616): Ariel's Song from Act 5,
Scene 1, lines 88-93, of *The Tempest* (1611).

Jo Shapcott: "Life" from *My Life Asleep* (OUP, 1998). Her
last collection was *Tender Taxes* (Faber, 2002), being versions
of Rainer Maria Rilke's poems. *Her Book: Poems 1988-1998*
was published by Faber in 1999. In 1996, with Matthew
Sweeney, she edited the anthology *Emergency Kit*.
BY PERMISSION OF FABER.

Penelope Shuttle: "The Bat of Totality" from *Redgrove's
Wife* (Bloodaxe, 2006). She has published five collections since
1980 including a *Selected Poems* in 1998. She was married to
the poet Peter Redgrove who died in 2003. *Redgrove's Wife* was
shortlisted for the 2007 Forward Prize.
BY PERMISSION OF THE AUTHOR AND DAVID HIGHAM
ASSOCIATES.

(Dame) **Edith Sitwell** (1884-1964): "The Bat" from *Facade,*
a sequence of poems written for William Walton's music and
first performed in 1922. A champion of many young writers,
her *Collected Poems* was published by MacMillan in 1957.
BY PERMISSION OF DAVID HIGHAM ASSOCIATES.

Stevie Smith (1902-1971): "The Fairy Bell" from *Collected
Poems* (MacMillan, 1975). She published seven collections and,
in 1936, a book of fiction, *Novel on Yellow Paper*.

She was awarded the Queen's Gold Medal for Poetry, in 1969.
BY PERMISSION OF THE ESTATE OF JAMIE MACGIBBON.

Matthew Sweeney: "The Bats" from *The Lame Waltzer* (Allison and Busby, 1985). His *Selected Poems* was published in 2002. He has published eleven collections, the latest being *Black Moon* (Cape Poetry, 2007). He edited *The New Faber Book of Children's Poems*, two other anthologies and a new collected poems of Walter de la Mare.
BY PERMISSION OF THE AUTHOR AND RANDOM HOUSE GROUP.

John Tranter: "Bats" from *New and Selected Poems* (University of Queensland Press and Salt Publishing, 2006). He has published seven collections. Edited *The Bloodaxe Book of Modern Australian Poetry* (Bloodaxe, 1992), and edits the internet poetry magazine, *Jacket*.
BY PERMISSION OF THE AUTHOR AND SALT.

John Updike: "Zoo Bats" from his *Collected Poems 1953-1993,* published by Alfred Knopf in 1993. A prolific novelist, also author of short stories and critical essays. He won the Pulitzer Prize for Fiction.
BY PERMISSION OF CURTIS BROWN LTD.

Susan Wicks: "Protected Species" from *The Clever Daughter* (Faber, 1996). *Her Night Toad — New and Selected Poems* was published by Bloodaxe in 2003. Her new collection is *De-Iced* (Bloodaxe, 2007).
BY PERMISSION OF FABER.

Richard Wilbur. "Mind" from *Things Of This World* (Harcourt Brace, 1956). His *Collected Poems* was published by Waywiser Press in 2006. He has received numerous awards for poetry and translation and was the second Poet Laureate of the USA in 1987.
BY PERMISSION OF WAYWISER PRESS.

Tamar Yoseloff: was born in the US in 1965. Her first collection, *Sweetheart* (Slow Dancer, 1998) was a PBS Special

Commendation and the winner of the Aldeburgh Festival Prize. Her second collection, *Barnard's Star*, was published by Enitharmon in 2004. Her latest book, *Fetch*, is published by Salt in 2007, as well as *Marks*, a collaborative book with the artist Linda Karshan, published by Pratt Contemporary Art.

Michael Baron initiated the major Words By The Water Cumbrian Literature Festival in 2001, and is closely involved with writing and promoting "the word" in that County. He is also a member of the Cumberland Bat Group, and of the Bat Conservation Trust. In 1962 he was one of the founders of the National Autistic Society, and was awarded the M.B.E. for services to autism.

*Despite every effort, in a few cases, we have been unable to trace the copyright holders prior to publication. The publisher will be pleased to rectify any errors or omissions in any later editions.

Royalties from this book are donated to the Bat Conservation Trust

The Bat Conservation Trust (BCT) is the only UK charity solely devoted to conserving bats and their habitats. BCT is working towards a world where bats and people live in harmony, and aims to secure and enhance bat populations for future generations to enjoy.

Bat Conservation Trust

www.bats.org.uk
Bat Helpline:
0845 1300 228

***

Also available from Five Leaves

Not Just a Game: sporting poetry
Edited by Andy Croft and Sue Dymoke
225 pages, 978 1 905512 13 3, £9.99 paperback

From the first length to the final frame, from Jack Hobbs to Brian Clough, from Centre Court to the Great North Run, *Not Just a Game* captures the tension and the laughter, the pain and the pleasure, and the blood sweat and tears. A unique archive of sporting life — from angling to boxing, from swimming to tennis, from cricket to football and back again, and from hang-gliding to skittleball, as recorded by John Betjeman, UA Fanthorpe, Seamus Heaney, Ted Hughes, PG Wodehouse, John Arlott and many more.

Post-free on www.inpressbooks.co.uk/fiveleaves